A Musician Talks

I. THE INTEGRITY OF MUSIC

A Musician Talks

1. THE INTEGRITY OF MUSIC

By

Donald Francis Tovey

Oxford University Press

LONDON NEW YORK TORONTO

OXFORD UNIVERSITY PRESS
AMEN HOUSE, E.C. 4
LONDON   EDINBURGH   GLASGOW
NEW YORK   TORONTO   MELBOURNE
CAPETOWN   BOMBAY   CALCUTTA
MADRAS
GEOFFREY CUMBERLEGE
PUBLISHER TO THE
UNIVERSITY

First Impression   1941
Second Impression 1942
Third Impression 1946

PRINTED IN GREAT BRITAIN

EDITOR'S NOTE

DONALD FRANCIS TOVEY was invited in 1936 by the University of Glasgow to deliver the Cramb Lectures, and in 1938 by the University of Liverpool to deliver the Alsop Lectures. University Lectures, daily or occasional, provided a medium in which Tovey felt comfortable, and these courses gave him an equal pleasure and incentive to express his ideas.

In prose-writing Tovey worked at his best with the printer's devil at his elbow. Not one of his now famous programme analyses had its origin save in a performance, not even from the days of the Meiningen Orchestra. He projected a number of books and editions. Yet of his published works only one, as far as I know, was the result of ignition without the tinder of performance—and that one was not entirely the result of spontaneous combustion. I refer to the *Companion to the Art of Fugue*. Even the cadenzas to classical concertos and the redistribution of the Haydn trios could trace a lineage from actual concerts, and the *Companion* would never have been written had not Tovey delighted in playing the last Fugue of *Die Kunst der Fuge* with his own superlative ending.

For the appearance of these two volumes, issued under the name of *A Musician Talks*, I am partly responsible. To an extent Tovey needed his books to be made for him. One of the projects mentioned above was planned to fill a big frame. It was a series

v

of text-books on music, to comprehend his own system of musical education. Their subjects were to be Counterpoint, Thorough-Bass, Form, and Orchestration. Not a word of them was ever written down. The scheme, however, simmered in his brain, and was after some years reduced to two composite books by his own wish. Still pen was not put to paper. Then came the call of the lectures, and at last Tovey, having accepted the invitations, was obliged to produce the matter in prose.

He dictated the lectures to his secretary and allowed the duplicate of the typescript to go to the printer and to be set up in type. But only those who were present at the delivery of the lectures can by comparison with this text have a real sense of how Tovey illuminated his words with the magic of his pianoforte playing. That a large part of the lectures was occupied by music is obvious: not only were there many long passages from the classical composers, but there were long improvisations in one style or another (cf. p. 27 of 'Musical Textures', where the lecturer showed how Klengel might have treated a given fugue subject).

On receiving his proofs Tovey was a little doubtful what to do about musical examples, as he was about the obvious overlapping of the two books in certain arguments and illustrations. To quote at anything like the length required would have turned a book into an album of music with annotations. But it was soon agreed that minor adjustments would avoid long citation. The overlapping I made light of, and Tovey also agreed to the issue of the books under the informal title they now bear. All was ready, but he was no diligent proof-reader, and he never corrected the proofs himself.

On his death, Lady Tovey kindly gave her consent to the publication of the books as they now stand. Also with her consent I invited Dr. Ernest Walker to contribute a Preface and give the proofs a final approval. The text exactly follows Tovey's words except for the main title, and except that certain small circumlocutions have been necessary, as I have explained above, to avoid musical examples, and certain corrections where the prose style betrayed dictation and lack of later revision. But I can testify that they are less in number than Tovey himself would probably have made.

For one admirer, at least, repetitions are but a slight disadvantage against the enormous advantage of the possession of two more of Tovey's writings.

HUBERT J. FOSS

November 1940.

PREFACE

DONALD FRANCIS TOVEY was born at Eton on 17 July 1875 and died at Edinburgh on 10 July 1940. My own acquaintance dates from October 1894, when he came up to Balliol as the first holder of the Lewis Nettleship Musical Scholarship: an undergraduate whose age was the only ordinary thing about him. With a winning personality keenly appreciative of the humorous, and abundant non-musical interests, he dropped easily into normal college life; but he had never been to a school of any kind, and had from early childhood been privately trained for the musical profession. There were other musically minded undergraduates in Oxford, but Tovey was very obviously in a class altogether by himself; not only was he an outstanding pianist, but the Bach-Gesellschaft scores were his regular bedside literature, and he had written full-dress symphonies—I still recall the opening page of one in E minor, and its author's innocent pleasure in the subtly artistic snag of the reiterated wind chords which, until the entry of the violins, suggested that the key was F major. A finely equipped musician in practice and in theory, the youth was father to the man. Tovey was a three-fold artist: in performance, in creation, in knowledge.

It was as a notably artistic pianist, in chamber music as well as in solo work, that Tovey was first generally known to the public: and throughout his life pianism, including problems of technique as well as of interpretation, remained a prominent though gradually a less absorbing interest. Among my own memories perhaps the most vivid are those of performances of the late Beethoven Sonatas, particularly op. 101 and op. 111: these were, very masterfully, the real thing. He was very versatile: Scriabin and Brucken-Fock and Hindemith had their turns as well as the classics. Line-drawing was nearer to his heart than niceties of colour; but anyhow it was always playing in the big manner, absolutely faithful and with finely modelled phrasing and a rhythm that could bend but never break. In his conducting, also, I always felt the same sure judgement of tempo; though he seemed less at home with London orchestras than with his more personally familiar Edinburgh folk.

Notwithstanding that he could complete Bach's *Kunst der Fuge* with dazzling certainty of style and technique, and write concerto-cadenzas that Beethoven and Brahms would have been glad to father, Tovey had as a composer a definite style of his own; and it changed little in essentials throughout his published work, from the op. 1 B minor Pianoforte Trio (dedicated to Parry as 'the first work of a grateful pupil') down to the end. In his earlier and more leisured life he was prolific; but after, in 1914, he had accepted the Reid Professorship of Music in the University of Edinburgh, and added to his other activities those of the busy and inspiring teacher and orchestral trainer, his output slackened a great deal. From time to time he showed me things that have, so far as I know, remained fragments; in these twenty-five years he produced for publication only two works, the choral setting of the Northumbrian 'Lyke-Wake Dirge', a miniature but none the less outstanding masterpiece full of a strange sombre beauty, and the spacious Violoncello Concerto, the finely massive first movement of which best, perhaps, represents his instrumental achievements. Otherwise I would direct special attention to the great closing scene of the opera *The Bride of Dionysus* (pre-1914, though not performed until later), the Variations for string quartet often played by the Busch Ensemble, the E minor Quartet for pianoforte and strings, the D major Pianoforte Trio (which I have heard its composer mention as if it were a rather favourite child), or, in lighter vein, the 'Balliol Dances' for pianoforte duet—the first five dating from undergraduate days, the remainder from considerably later. To the neophyte, these duets are the best of initiations into Tovey's compositions: we may feel the hand of Brahms in No. 5, but it is only a passing touch, and the transition from the penultimate to the last of the Dances is one of the most personal, and one of the most beautiful, things Tovey ever wrote. Though as a rule very quick in his literary work, he was a slow composer; and he suffered, possibly to his detriment, from a certain inability to leave a work alone when completed and performed, or even, in the case of the opera, when published. He could not, so to speak, refrain from fingering his creativeness. None the less, the creativeness is there.

It is, however, as a writer about rather than of music that Tovey has, at any rate up to the present, enjoyed the widest fame. He had read and remembered in detail and, what is more, methodically assimilated into his personal scheme of aesthetics, every page of live music from Byrd and Lassus and Palestrina to the end of the nineteenth century, with a great and varied mass of twentieth-century music in addition. The live music, I say; he was not the kind of scholar who is interested in a fact simply as a fact, and about dead music he did not worry. But he was not pedantically exclusive; some second-rank composers such as Méhul he had studied with minuteness, and he knew all that need be known about even third-rate folk. Unlike his Edinburgh predecessor and intimate friend, Frederick Niecks, he was not interested in composers' biographies: he knew Beethoven's works backwards, but cared nothing for his life—and less than nothing for attempts to correlate his music with the French Revolution. Definite artistic achievement of some kind was what mainly attracted him. He did not pay any very special attention to even creditable composers who, in his judgement, were merely pioneers or gap-bridgers: though his active dislikes were few— Saint-Saëns ('slick classicism' and 'thin, mundane lucidity') and, to a less extent, Liszt. Even then, he was catholic-minded enough to perform the Symphonic Poems of the former ('they are so damned clever'): and he was fond of Liszt's 'Orpheus', while often playing his transcriptions of Beethoven's Symphonies with enthusiastically admiring running comments.

Tovey was a brilliant talker: unfortunately he lacked a Boswell. But he often wrote in the same way that he talked; and we have from his pen six volumes of analytical essays, many elaborate articles in the *Encyclopedia Britannica*, the long essays on Brahms and Haydn in Cobbett's *Cyclopedic Survey of Chamber Music*, annotated editions of Bach and Beethoven, pamphlets, and many sporadic articles in journals and composite books, with various lectures —the Edinburgh inaugural, the Deneke and Romanes lectures at Oxford, the Hertz British Academy Lecture, and the Alsop and Cramb lectures first printed in these volumes. It is by these many hundreds of pages that he has achieved a world reputation; and, indeed, there is nothing like it all in English nor, so far as I know, in any other language. Perhaps we see the quintessence of his thought most completely in the Philip Maurice Deneke lecture on 'Musical Form and Matter', delivered at Lady Margaret Hall, Oxford, in June 1934: the germ from which the Cramb lectures in the present volumes have developed.

A great man must have his diversions; and, as all his acquaintances remember, Tovey had, all through his life, the keenest of appetites for wit, humour, and frank nonsense. The poetry of Edward Lear, Lewis Carroll, Hilaire Belloc, he knew by heart, set to brilliantly suitable music (unfortunately never written down), and sang *con amore*, along with advertisements, extracts from *Punch*, and so on *ad infinitum*; and in later life he added the *Galgenlieder* of Christian Morgenstern to his repertoire, though, I think, only for non-musical recitation. And, in one way or another, the same trait peeps out—or perhaps jumps out—in many a page of his critical writings: the index to his volumes of analytical essays, the last thing that he personally passed for press, contains entries that are nothing less than impish. A great man's diversions may often, to merely casual eyes, loom larger than they really are. With Tovey, anyhow, no one would have wished them otherwise. But as diversions they are a remembrance that will pass : it is the greatness that remains.

ERNEST WALKER

These Lectures were delivered in the University of Glasgow in November and December 1936, with the kind assistance of Professor W. Gillies Whittaker, M.A., D.Mus., F.R.C.O., who made the arrangements in connection therewith.

Much of the Preface has already appeared in the pages of *The Monthly Musical Record*, and thanks are due to the Editor for kindly allowing this reprint.

CONTENTS

LECTURE I

THE musical doctrine which I wish to illustrate in the present course of lectures was adumbrated by me in the summer of 1934 in one of the Philip Maurice Deneke lectures at Oxford. In spite of its discursive form, and even in spite of its apparent digressions, that lecture suffers from over-compression, and I always intended to make it the basis of a more systematic illustration of its subject. Hence I am specially grateful to the Cramb Trustees for honouring me by an invitation which enables me to execute this plan.

My general title, 'The Integrity of Music', may be presumed to explain itself. It indicates that music is a special illustration of the integrity of art in general. This is no vague proposition. It implies an essential difference between art and science. The task of my first lecture will be to illustrate this difference and to show that herein music has no special privileges against other arts. For this reason I have much to say before I come to definitely musical topics. The question is not merely academic. It is vitally practical and contemporary. In every period of art only a small fraction of what is produced is destined to survive to later ages, and that fraction could not have been produced without the environment which produced all the rest. Criticism might conceivably be organized on lines scientific enough to allow it to predict in terms of an actuary's tables what percentage of contemporary art would survive, but contemporary criticism has always been as helpless as an actuary when it has tried to select individual works for immortality.

To-day no sane person doubts that John Sebastian Bach is one of the greatest masters of any art that has ever lived. But no competent musical historian who honestly examines the strength of his own musical faith can suppose that if he had been a pupil of John Sebastian Bach he would have predicted the immortality of his master's works. We may hope that in such a position we should have had an irresistible conviction that for us this was the greatest music in the world; but the master himself was quite cheerful in his acceptance of the fact that such music no longer appealed to modern ears; and instead of deploring the degeneracy of the times, he said that the art had advanced to great heights, implying without bitterness that this was why his own music appealed to nobody. If any actual pupil of Bach understood him as we can, his only possible conclusion would be that for him this was the greatest music in the world, but that such was his private opinion, and *de gustibus non est disputandum*.

Such practical wisdom may seem cold, but it is at all events sane. Sanity adapts itself to its environment and minds its own business. Insanity both shuts itself up in a box and tries to convert the world to its private views. And herein lies the most serious practical importance of the distinction between science and art. Most of the perishable and decadent elements in art have been in existence at all periods, and our illusion that they are especially modern arises from our total lack of interest in the forms they have

2

taken in works we have willingly let die. But it seems probable that modern art has suffered especially from tendencies to confuse its modes of thought with those of science. Only one thing can save the results of such a tendency from being foredoomed: and that is the very fact that, whatever the official propaganda of an artist may be, neither art nor science can make a work of art into a scientific product. The artist's scientific theories are for the most part too half-baked to detain a man of science for five minutes, and the man of science who will allow himself to be so detained by an artist will have very little conception of the meaning of art. If a theory of art helps the artist to compose, it does not matter whether it is correct, pseudo-scientific, or naïvely representational and everything else that modern criticism abhors.

A correct theory of art is seldom, if ever, a guarantee or even a help to the artist in the creating and perfecting of his work. It is not unscientific for a doctor to ask his patient to 'say. 99'. It is not even unscientific to base a successful slum practice on faith and bottles of coloured tisanes. The doctor's scientific and medical object is to provoke the right reactions in the patient. Modern pseudo-scientific theories, and the classical art-forms themselves, have been serviceable in stimulating the right activity in the artist. Pedantry and quackery begin when our ninety-nines and tinctures are erected into magical devices that annoy the public and become sacred causes of martyrdom to the artist.

The first step towards understanding the integrity of art is to recognize that it consists in the integrity of each individual work of art; that, as I have

3

expressed it elsewhere, there is no such thing as Art with a capital A. Bach was too modest if he thought that his own music could be superseded by a new art that 'had risen to great heights'. You note that even in this connexion he did not use the word 'progress'. That is a word certainly applicable to science, but almost invariably misleading when applied to art. Science with a capital S does exist as a body of organized knowledge with a definite aim. That definite aim is knowledge of the universe and is not to be frustrated by the certainty that it will never be attained, nor even by the tendency of some philosophers to cast doubts upon whether a universe in the strict sense of the term exists. The man of science must not only work in the belief that the universe does cohere as a whole, but he must be content with no lesser wholeness and must regard with grave suspicion any scientific theory which has the kind of completeness that pleases the artist. Helmholtz has some illuminating remarks on Goethe's scientific work. His criticism comes to this: that Goethe could make important discoveries in morphology because he had the artist's view of phenomena that concern concrete and relatively detachable objects; but that he was helpless and recalcitrant in scientific work on the phenomena of light, which are diffused over the whole universe and become more and more abstractly mathematical and metaphysical the more deeply they are studied. Goethe was prouder of his theory of colour than of any other work, artistic, diplomatic, or scientific, that he had achieved. Helmholtz points out that that theory is an admirable description of appearances and has precisely the qualities of observation that made Goethe a pioneer of evolution in botany and anatomy. But as a scientific theory it is as unintelligible to men of science as Newton's methods were unintelligible to Goethe, whose attacks upon Newton show that he is really bewildered to the verge of a nervous crisis by a man of science whose optical theories are so outrageously unsuggestive of what colour looks like.

The duty of the man of science is, then, to contribute to the body of knowledge called Science. In order to make his task practicable, he must isolate and confine his problem within narrow categories. He must work under laboratory conditions and must not confuse one science with another. Aesthetic prejudices must not interfere with his optics, and if his political economy is to be a science at all he must not let ethical ideas intrude nor deviate from political economy into politics and housekeeping. On the other hand, he must be prepared for the time when the subjects of his observations and experiments are to be released from their immediate laboratory conditions. Roughly speaking, the more the subjects of his science are removed from the world that satisfies the artist, the easier and safer is the scientific abstraction. Physical science is becoming more and more mathematical, not without causing symptoms of disquiet lest its applications of mathematics should outrun its discretion. But pure mathematics is not obliged to wait for physical science to keep step with it. The mathematicians proceed at their own discretion within their own category.

It would be crude to say that the artist's method is the exact opposite of that of science; but the comparing of opposite characters is the clearest way to show the difference. Moreover, it brings out the resemblances between science and art, without which there would have been neither danger of confusion nor the possibility of an intellectual pleasure in qualities common to both. Some philosophic tendencies may, with or without the intention of their promoters, shake what faith we have in the unity of the universe. There is no difficulty in believing in the unity of a convincing work of art. I cannot say whether there is any widespread belief that the individual work of art is a microcosm; but such is my own belief, and music, which has no motive for being anything but an art, is remarkably rich in examples. A work of art, in as far as its purpose is unmixed, is a single coherent whole, and as such expresses our faith in the possibility of wholeness and coherence. This conception is a first step towards the view that artistic wholeness or perfection is a type of infinity.

Before any premature objection can be raised, let us note that there is nothing in the nature of art and of its materials to make artistic perfection impossible. The elements of art are selected by human beings, and its problems are completely under human control. Many further difficulties also may be swept away by postulating that artistic wholeness may be recognized in less than the whole. Art is in this respect no worse off than science, which is committed to assume both that the universe will always make sense and that we shall never make sense of it. There is nothing to prevent scientific truths from entering into a work of art if the work is large enough for them.

There are very few straight lines or perfect circles in nature, but there is one, the horizon, which will be visible in every wide prospect and which is implied in every correct perspective. Accordingly, if pictorial art chooses to include the common but interesting human experience of perspective, it must include so much optical geometry as is inherent in the way in which we all use our eyes. But the pictorial artist must command a wide prospect before the horizon will present itself directly to him as a straight line to be expressed as such in his picture. In fact, to see the horizon amounts to seeing, at least by inference, the dome of the sky, and hence to seeing our first view of the universe. This illustration is a useful symbol of the way in which some features of a work of art may be recognizable as scientific elements without destroying the art, and I am sometimes tempted to use the word 'straight' as a symbol of such cases. The most important of these are grouped round the science or art of logic. Art can no more exist without it than science: but though it is the master of science, it must be kept in its place as the butler of art. One hears a great deal about logical development in music, and both in the analysis of the classics and in the teaching of composition this term covers some of the most dangerous fallacies in popular and academic aesthetics. You cannot get rid of logic any more than you can get rid of the horizon, but the occasions in which logic appears on the surface are as rare in music as in any art which selects an artistic sufficiency of human experience for its purposes. Here, again, if your work of art is large enough, its logical coherence will appear on the surface to about the same extent as it will appear in any actual human experience of equal calibre. The most familiar and extensive appearance of crude logic in modern literature is shown in the detective story, where the logical sequence is usually inverted, its conclusion being first presented as a mystery of which the explanation is disclosed in reverse order of events. This logical dictatorship restricts the detective story from the range and depth of less mathematical forms of literature.

Artistic range and depth must be human, and they need not become less human as they become more abstract. If this were not so, pure instrumental music would be the coldest of arts: whereas those who understand it find it more intense than any other. Neither abstruse thought nor rarefied atmosphere is to be mistaken for the intrusion of science into art. They may represent human experiences as artistically as a lifelike character study of a man of science. Those who can appreciate the works of Henry James find no loss, but a gain in human interest in his progress from the early novels which could be ended by a tragic fall from a cliff to novels which tell how A's partial misconception of B's undecided impression of A's attitude towards C impelled A to offer B a cigar. Think as you will of the taste which enjoys such subtleties, neither the selection nor the treatment of the subject points to anything but purely artistic principles. Science has not intruded, and the reactions are not produced under laboratory conditions.

It is the duty of the man of science to let no sentimental or aesthetic interests interfere with his work. His first duty towards his own theories is to try to disprove them. I heard the discoverer of argon and other inert gases explain that he was led to his discoveries by one of the first principles of scientific measurement: viz. Never remove a discrepancy. Another aspect of this precept would be: Never add a pinch of salt to taste. It is obvious that the artist habitually perfects his work by removing discrepancies and adding what is needed for no other purposes than those of taste. Moreover, his selection of materials always makes a world complete in itself and not analysed into categories. The most rarefied of Henry James's later works not only presupposes a highly complex and refined civilization, but gives abundant evidence that such a civilization coheres in his mind, more perfectly than anything like it in the outer world. Such evidence is a vital necessity to works of art. To take an example of Henry James's middle period, it is not merely what Maisie knew, but what everyone knows that holds that novel together. In the last resort, no matter how works of art may have depended on their environment before they could be produced at all, once a genuine work of art has been created it carries enough of its environment with it to explain itself to future and foreign civilizations.

My favourite illustrations of this were forced upon me in my undergraduate days when I was trying to cram up enough classics to satisfy examiners who did not profess to be interested in music. Homer's civilization evidently differs considerably from that of Oxford; but this makes no difference to the vividness or even to the actuality of what he describes. Alcinous greets Odysseus with delight on finding

9

that he is the famous pirate and sacker of cities, instead of being, as he had suspected, one of those confounded merchantmen. There may have been a Homeric age in which this had the charm of a realistic trait. It now has a romantic charm just because its point of view would be disavowed by our own Royal Family. The proposition that nothing is true which a change of date can make false is perhaps the most fundamental of all aesthetic rules. The *Odyssey* remains irrefutable not because we must accept its estimate of the social status of pirates, but because it makes that estimate perfectly clear instead of taking it for granted. In those remote days of my attempts to penetrate through thick blankets of 'crib' to the original Greek, I encountered in Sophocles another point of view which, according to Mr. Bernard Shaw and many of my Oxford contemporaries, was too obsolete to have for us the tragic value that it had for Sophocles. I was told that we do not think of funerals as Antigone did. Hence it was held that the cause of Antigone's martyrdom had to modern taste an unfortunate resemblance to the taste of the little seaport which, according to Tennyson, gave the strong soul of Enoch Arden the costliest funeral within its records. I have never been able to accept this criticism. To me Tennyson has not unmistakably risen beyond a tenderly humorous patronage of the villagers' simple faith. Such patronage, even if humorous, is apt to jar without achieving irony; and in any case, like all patronage, it puts the artist hopelessly outside his work. In the case of Antigone, it always seemed to me evident that her belief in the duty of burying her brother was a tragic necessity of central importance in her universe, and that it was as impertinent to accuse Sophocles for talking Greek instead of rising to the language of my cribs as to compare the cause of Antigone's martyrdom with even the real pathos of the comfort which our poorer classes derive from a sumptuous funeral. Antigone's belief and its origins are, in fact, neither taken for granted nor presented as novelties. They are presented with the same enthusiasm for actuality as that with which Pepys writes in his *Diary* that the watchman called out the time 'as I was penning this very line'.

My luck ordained that I had to read the *Ajax* at the same time as I read the *Antigone*, and here I found an obvious instance of the way in which a contemporary feature in a work of art may be so presented as not to stand a change of climate. After the tragedy of Ajax himself is over, there is a long wrangle between Odysseus and other heroes as to whether Ajax's conduct has entitled him to an honourable funeral. The mere position of this topic makes it for us an anticlimax to be explained only by the force of beliefs that have lost their force for us; and it is evident that their force for the characters of the drama is that of a jealousy essentially unheroic and mean, or, at best, the jealousy of a technical orthodoxy. I have never since found a clearer illustration of the difference between the art that can keep its subjects alive throughout future ages and an art which has left some part of its material in a perishable state.

A work of art can never be superseded. With architecture, sculpture, and painting, time brings physical decay for which the artist is not to blame, unless for the sake of immediate effect he knowingly uses short-lived materials. Replicas and copies may be good enough to make the record of the artist's creations immune from the ravages of time, and the aesthetic value of a copy that can deceive the un-aided eye of the expert is at least equal to that of great music perfectly played. The truth must be faced that music exists only in performance. No musician will agree to this in any sense that would impel him to confine his experience to what he has leisure and opportunity for hearing; a competent musical scholar must have read and enjoyed with all the pleasures of imagination incalculably more music than he will hear in a lifetime, and his knowledge of works that he has actually heard would need many more hearings before it could attain the depth and clearness of what he can gain by reading them. But his imagination depends upon memory, and it is per-formance, not technical abstractions, that he imagines when he reads. It is an immense advantage to music that the value of the autograph is mainly sentimental. This removes from the category of musical aesthetics a large number of issues that complicate—we might even say, confuse—the judgements of connoisseurs of painting and sculpture. Far be it from me to deny the unique value of the original painting; but, to take one notorious case, my sympathies are entirely with Professor Bode in the tragedy of his insistence that a translation of *La Gioconda* into the terms of a wax bust was the authentic work of Leonardo. Bode was not alone among museum directors in thinking that this wax bust was a very beautiful thing. His only mistake was in assuming that a skilled craftsman cannot execute a masterly translation of a work that he could not have created. If the training of Sir Walter Parratt has conferred upon an organist the habit of playing a toccata of Bach perfectly in a noble style, his performance will not give me any certainty that his own compositions, or even his own general musicianship, may not be as commonplace as the roll of Victorian quilt that was found to be the core of Ralph Cockle Lucas's *Gioconda*.

The perfection of works of art is not only a question separable from external accidents. It is a quality inherent in the very conception of art, as I have already implied in suggesting that the individual work of art is a microcosm. The conditions of music are specially favourable to the actual attaining of perfection: indeed, Schweitzer goes so far as to say that there is no other art in which perfection is so necessary to the permanent value of the work. The circumstances are indeed rare in which music has any but purely artistic motives for existing; and, whereas some of the greatest monuments of literature, such as the *Aeneid*, have openly professed a patriotic or instructive purpose, most of the music that has professed anything of the kind is so poor that no composer can have any ambition to write music that will play a part in general history.

Such is the normal purity of music that it tempts the critic into many fallacies of narrowness and over-simplification. With these I must deal more fully in my next lecture. For the present, let us understand that the integrity of music—or, if you prefer it, the purity of music—in no way depends on the absence of non-musical elements in the art. The most perfect, as well as the most ancient, of musical instruments is the human voice; and the human voice is normally used for human speech. Music loses none of its integrity by allowing the singing voice to utter words. The art of reconciling the claims of words with those of musical form is not simple, but neither is it impure. Apart from dance music, the main stream of musical thought originated in voices, and always advanced as an art of treating words, allowing only small scope for inarticulate vocalizing.

Not only is it impossible to think away the original rhetorical associations of music, but it is necessary to use them as criteria for even the most absolute instrumental music. If I had entitled the present course of lectures 'The Purity of Music', I might have eventually proved by logic that musical purity does not depend upon the absence of extra-musical elements and conditions; but the proof would have been laboured, and would not have outweighed the prejudices and doctrines that have cramped the musical ideas of many critics and of some composers. It is more practical to regard purity as a question-begging epithet. The word 'integrity' serves all the purposes that can be served by the word 'purity', and it allows us to consider profitable and thoroughly artistic questions about the way in which the arts can integrate a combination of their resources and of all that their material naturally suggests. Unless such an integration is allowed as a normal condition of art, our notion of purity will suffer from what is essentially a confusion between art and science. Only a scientific habit of abstraction could tolerate the view that the musical use of the voice should be dissociated from words; or that words, once admitted in music, should not be treated illustratively. The integrity of music is not preserved, but injured, by a less-than-human use of the voice; and some of you may be horrified to find that I regard Wagner as an artist who preserved the integrity of music as meticulously as Mozart. Programme music—that is to say, instrumental music unassociated with the stage, but gratuitously illustrating non-musical matters—is obviously the field in which musical integrity is most exposed to doubt; for there is no inherent necessity for it. Beethoven once said that he always composed according to some *Bild* that he had in his mind, and this remark reverberates through the ages as a summons to that kind of inattention which enables people who are not very fond of music to while away the time while a symphony is in progress. When the German word *Bild* is translated as 'picture', Beethoven's meaning is absurdly narrow. The word means little more than 'idea'; in fact, it does mean precisely 'idea' as Plato would have conceived it and is a happy instance of the genius of the German language for translating Greek terms accurately.

A still more significant point in Beethoven's confession is that he not only seldom told us what the *Bild* was, but was as rude to people who inquired about it as any of us are inclined to be to intrusions upon our private affairs. Beethoven's rudeness is justified by the cataracts of hasty criticism that have fallen upon the few important works in which he has given a name to his *Bilder*. Any popularity that his 'Pastoral'

Symphony may at one time have owed to its title has been forgotten or adduced as evidence against it by criticisms which show a brutal inability to understand it on its musical merits. The real and avowed inspiring occasion of the sonata *Les Adieux, l'Absence, et le Retour* is not romantic enough for the sentimental people to whom titles are necessary for the enjoyment of music; and so it has not even had the benefit of the cheap popularity that is brought in evidence against the 'Pastoral' Symphony, as an offset against the difficulties of its being one of Beethoven's most subtle and unusual works. In my next lecture I shall deal in more detail with the conditions of absolute music and absolute arts. Let us at present sum up the general position.

From the romanticism that pervaded most of the nineteenth century down to very recent times, programme music has tended more and more to crowd absolute music out of the field. The only objection to it is that there is no inherent necessity for instrumental music to have a programme. On the other hand, the pictorial plastic arts, and latterly even poetry itself, have developed almost a conscientious objection to anything but the most abstract treatment of their materials. It is even begging the question to speak of their materials. Outside the realms of abstract art, the material of human speech is human meaning; and you cannot proceed far or long in the handling of colours and forms without resembling natural objects in a way which, however accidental, must be distracting to the attention. No doubt it was long ago high time that not only critics, but the general public, should be drastically cured of the habit which sees and enjoys the subject, and nothing but the subject, of a picture, and it is certain that no conceivable predominance of programme music will ever reduce the general public to quite such an abject condition of seeing nothing in music except the subjects it pretends to illustrate. Music can afford a reckless extravagance in gratuitous illustration, and the other arts have doubtless needed a drastic remedy for the irrelevancies to which mere illustration betrayed them. Still, the fact remains that doctrines which insist on abstractness in painting and the use of words for their sounds rather than their sense are in essentials a confusion between science and art. They would be fallacious even if they were scientific; but the real man of science knows better. When he believes that a line is length without breadth he is under no delusion that there is any such thing in nature or art; but it is by no means clear that the artists who act upon an *a priori* abstract theory of art have any correct notion of even what an abstraction really means. It is one thing to see the fallacy of a criticism which ignores every aspect of a picture except those by which it illustrates its subject, but it is not legitimate to proceed from this to demand that the artist should shut himself into a world in which colours and forms abstain from behaving on his canvas as they behave in real life. That way madness lies; or something too much like it to be worth the trouble of distinguishing from it.

My first propositions, then, are as follows:

Science is not art, and, if a work of art can legitimately convey scientific information, that is because its material includes matters of universal scope.

C   17

Thus, for example, a whole landscape may be divided horizontally by a straight line if that straight line represents the horizon.

Secondly, a correct theory of art is not necessarily a practical method of producing works of art, any more than it is an element likely to appear explicitly in the result. It concerns criticism, not creation.

Thirdly, art consists of individual works of art, not a general growing body of knowledge like science. The integrity of science implies that science is pursued for its own sake and not for practical purposes. The integrity of art is the integrity of works of art.

Fourthly, there is nothing to prevent a work of art from being perfect. Its perfection is only its highest standard of integrity, and its integrity can be secured by the artist's choice of his materials.

Fifthly, if the artist has omitted no essential elements, his work will remain unaffected by changes in public opinion. Perhaps there was a time when Homer seemed realistic, there doubtless was a time when he seemed barbarous, and there will always be a time when he seems romantic. The difference between the three points of view is negligible. The thrill given by complete artistic integrity is always the same. The only things that change are the directions and difficulties through which we approach the work.

Sixthly, a work of art exists, as Andrew Bradley said of poetry, in countless degrees. For the most part its enjoyment cannot be a single experience, but must come from the accumulation in the memory of many and varied impressions. Music cannot properly be said to exist except in performance; and in this sense the authenticity of a piece of music can be preserved only when the performance respects the intentions of the composer and is otherwise adequate. The authenticity of the autograph is not an aesthetic factor at all; all that matters is proof of the faithfulness of copies. This is a general truth which ought to be faced by all connoisseurs of painting and sculpture to whom it may be unpalatable.

Seventhly, the integrity of an art is not preserved, but injured, by the exclusion of elements which cannot naturally be separated from its mean of existence. Pure instrumental music has so little reason to be otherwise than absolute that there is a strong presumption against the integrity of music that illustrates other subjects without the necessity forced upon it by the human voice or the stage. This presumption, however, is a difficulty that must be faced, not a prejudice that must be accepted. Absolute instrumental music is, as most musicians will agree, the highest form of the art; but it represents not more than the condition in which perfection is most easily attained and appreciated. Dean Church asserted that in literary criticism the terms 'higher' and 'lower' are unscientific; and, whatever may be the difficulties of attaining perfection in so highly compound an art as opera, we shall be well advised to avoid all criticism that implies that the art of opera is lower than that of the symphony or string quartet.

LECTURE II

WE need not wait until the question has been settled between those who wish art to be absolute and those who deny that such a consummation is possible or desirable. The beliefs which I wish to inculcate in these lectures are beliefs which I think practical as a basis for criticism and as a guide to creative and reproductive art.

In my first lecture I have pleaded for a large view of the integrity of music, and have explained that such integrity implies the integration of whatever elements are essential to the existence of the music. Such integrity is not preserved, but violated, by inhibiting the use of words in vocal music. The foundation of my entirely unoriginal and, I hope, common-sense doctrine was laid down for me in Andrew Bradley's inaugural lecture as Professor of Poetry at Oxford, in which, dealing with poetry for poetry's sake, he demonstrated with all the skill and soundness of an experienced philosopher that it is a fallacy that would separate the sound of words from their meaning. The fallacy is only apparently less crude than that which treats words as if their sound could be replaced without damage by that of any other words that literally and grammatically purport to describe the same objects. Let me borrow Bradley's shortest illustration, the difference between the words 'steed' and 'horse'. The dictionary can distinguish them only by distinguishing between a prose and a poetic vocabulary, and in bad poetry a 'steed' and a 'horse' are the same. But Byron could not interchange them when he wrote: ' "Bring me the horse." The horse was brought. In truth he was a noble steed'; though doubtless neither grammarian nor horse-coper can be very clear why he should not have said: ' "Bring me the steed." The steed was brought. In truth he was a noble horse.'

For purposes of analysis it may be convenient to abstract form from matter; and the matter of music, even where words are involved, is so remote from any other human experience that we are overwhelmingly tempted to regard most musical problems as problems of form, so long as we have any fear lest our analysis should degenerate into a mere popular account of external things alleged, rightly or wrongly, to be described by the music. Let us by all means beware of being distracted from music by the accidents of its resemblance to other things; but, in music as in poetry and the other arts, the opposite mistake is not much less crude: the mistake by which musical forms are conceived as mere jelly-moulds which determine the shape of music from outside. Not so has absolute music attained either its absoluteness or its supremacy in art. It has become untranslatable into other terms, but it has not become meaningless. On the contrary, it has become more exact than any language, as Mendelssohn pointed out in a remarkably profound letter which he courteously took the trouble to write to a tiresome person who asked him the meaning of some of his *Songs Without Words*. The inquiry was, perhaps, not so foolish as the people who have thought fit to supply those compositions with words, an absurdity that has been committed more than once. We need not be surprised that a person insensitive enough to commit it at all should show himself uniformly perverse in attaching the sentiments of merry Hussars on horseback to some of Mendelssohn's most melancholy pieces, and should represent Mendelssohn's perkiest cheerfulness by sweet maidenly meditations.

Perhaps it is not necessary to deal further with the intrusions of external matter upon musical substance. Such questions settle themselves without the need of special or technical knowledge; but it is important and by no means easy to determine how far the forms of music are inherent in musical matter. Let us be clear from the outset that, whatever objections we may raise to programme music, no pressure from external matter can violate the integrity of music more seriously than the pressure of an external form, though it profess itself to be purely musical. Now this is a matter in which not only appearances, but actual historical and practical processes, may be very deceptive. In fact, I do not believe that any *a priori* evidence can discriminate between a musical form that has been imposed from outside and one that has grown vitally and artistically from within. Of all the arts music is perhaps that in which art-forms are most easy to analyse and classify. Consequently, an immense amount of generalized knowledge about musical form has been accumulated, and has led inevitably to the view that the form exists before the music is composed. Rockstro's pious phrase, 'the rules to which the Great Masters gave their loving obedience', is one of the most dangerous heresies that has ever been accepted as an orthodoxy.

22

Quite apart from the fact that, as Dr. R. O. Morris has pointed out, Rockstro himself had to confess that he could often find no suitable illustration of these rules from the works of the great masters, the truth lies in precisely the opposite direction—viz. that where the rules have been intelligently drawn up they are the record of observers who devoted their loving and faithful observation to the practice of the great masters.

The rules which Rockstro had in mind were the grammatical rules of a musical dialect that attained its Attic, or Augustan, purity at the end of the sixteenth century. At that time the contemporary theorists were good observers, and students were ready to give the rules their loving obedience, because the whole tendency of music was towards a more and more fastidious purity and sense of euphony in the treatment of the unaccompanied chorus. Against my own principles I am shortening the argument by indulging in a special licence so as to speak of general tendencies instead of making the full statement that Palestrina and his greatest contemporaries found that fastidious attention to euphony was their greatest stimulus towards producing perfect individual works of art. The rules of strict counterpoint began to degenerate into an arbitrary and morbid casuistry when teachers refused to face the issue that in instrumental music these rules were true only in as far as instruments imitated the qualities of voices. A further step in the degeneration took place when teachers realized that the tonality of the Church modes was definitely obsolete, and that students must be trained in the more solid system of tonality

23

founded by Alessandro Scarlatti and pervading the whole musical art of the eighteenth and nineteenth centuries. The teachers of strict counterpoint then merely added the stiffness of modern tonality to the restrictions of pure sixteenth-century polyphony, entirely failing to see that those restrictions and the freedom and variety of the Church modes were intimately related. I believe it is still held by some teachers that students who are allowed to write strict counterpoint in the Church modes are thereby undermining their grasp of classical tonality. If a sense of classical tonality is to be represented by the harmonic style of our unrevised Victorian *Hymns Ancient and Modern*, it is difficult to see how any of the laxity of Palestrina's tonality could make a student's style worse. There is within the records of living memory the utterance of a venerable university don who would neither read Homer himself nor allow his pupils to read it, because such a study would be subversive of the standards of Attic Greek. This argues a very imperfect faith in the don's own capacity to retain his grasp of that noble dialect; and in any case it shows that his own education must be regarded as a total loss.

It is worth while dwelling upon the case of strict counterpoint, not merely because this is the narrowest and most unpopular of all items in musical education, but because, rightly understood, it shows the impossibility of separating technique from aesthetics. Just as it is convenient at times to disregard the integrity of the individual work of art and allow oneself to speak of general tendencies in music, so it may be convenient sometimes to say that such and such a problem is merely technical. In the same way, the astronomer talks of rising and setting and crossing the meridian, and of a planet as being stationary or retrograde in its orbit, just as if the Ptolemaic system were still accepted and nobody realized that these phenomena are merely the results of the earth's motion. But we must be not less careful than the astronomer to know when we are talking merely of phenomena and when we are dealing with what lies behind them. And it is significant that the greatest composers themselves have not only taken no trouble to separate technique from aesthetics, but have actually put forward some of their greatest works under the title of 'Exercises'. *Das Wohltemperirte Klavier* professes by its title to inculcate the tuning system of equal temperament for keyed instruments. The main bulk of the remainder of Bach's ripest keyboard works was published by him in five volumes under the title of *Klavierübung*. On the other hand, Domenico Scarlatti's sonatas show the same exalted view of technique in a negative way, for he published them with a preface warning the reader not to expect anything learned, but to regard them as written simply for his entertainment. Which is all the more remarkable since of all early keyboard music Scarlatti's sonatas notoriously make the most extravagant demands on the player's mechanical technique. But it is not even mechanical technique that is inseparable from aesthetics. Far more is it the case that nothing that concerns the composer as means to an end can be separated from that end.

Modern usage applies the term 'Studies', 'Übungen', or 'Etudes' to studies that inculcate technical mastery of an instrument—surely as low an aim as can be confessed by respectable artists. Even here English usage draws the line at calling such works 'exercises', though Bach himself and his early editors were less snobbish, and published the *Klavierübung* with the French title *Exercices pour le Clavecin*. It so happens that studies technically profitable to a player fall naturally into an art-form typified by some of Bach's most beautiful and characteristic preludes; a kind of musical network or lace, severely uniform in texture and rhythm, intolerant of anything obvious in the way of melody, but as capable of majestic growth and climax as a painter's finest studies in cloud perspective. Hence, there is no reason why *études* should not be great music. A goodly proportion of Chopin's twenty-seven *Études* are among his nobler works, and only three seem to me to be comparatively commonplace. The musical world was much disappointed when Debussy's collection of *études* turned out to be almost entirely preoccupied with dry, though eccentric, propositions.

It is not difficult to draw a line between pure aesthetics and these mechanical aspects of technique, and the only case in which confusion has arisen is that of the concerto. The orthodox view of concerto form has been fatally vulgarized by the assumption that the purpose of a concerto is to display the technique of the solo player. On this assumption concertos are, of course, ridiculously easy to write, and we need not wonder that the majority of them are hopelessly vulgar and trivial; but the true concerto forms and styles are represented by the highest and subtlest things in musical art, and their technical difficulty is the natural result of the condition that puts an individual player into the position of dominating an orchestra. But the real dangers of separating technique from aesthetics do not concern the skill of the player. I am not sure that Bach used the word *Übung* in any sense but that of 'exercise', but, like all his collected works, it happens also to be a series of studies in composition. However, the only work in which he avowed this has been more grossly misunderstood than anything else that he wrote. I refer to *Die Kunst der Fuge*, which is a series of fugues all on the same subject, classifying the main types of fugue and setting them forth in order of complexity; and here, by a specially annoying perversity, the fact that Bach wrote out this work in open score instead of on keyboard staves has led persons who have evidently never tried to play from score in their lives to assert that it is merely abstract music and so never meant to be played at all. I have not space to go into recent controversies about *Die Kunst der Fuge*, nor do I feel inclined to grumble because the belated recognition that that work has received has been displayed in forms which betray a scandalous prevalence of humbug in many accepted methods and schools of musical education.

Die Kunst der Fuge is, as its very title shows, an important *locus classicus* for the distinction between technique and aesthetics in so far as that distinction can represent facts. The whole work is founded on one subject. The task of showing all standard types of the treatment of that subject is in some cases a natural art-problem, and in some cases a discipline enforced. The subject must be capable of the most complex treatment, and it is therefore not free to have the qualities shown elsewhere by the subjects of Bach's simplest fugues. In *Die Kunst der Fuge* the fugues in which Bach is free to produce his finest music are those in which his severe main subject is combined with others. Even in the course of these Bach found himself faced by a contingency that had not occurred elsewhere in his experience. It was a mere accident that it had not occurred before; and Bach devoted the two most eccentric *tours de force* in *Die Kunst der Fuge* to working out a technique that would provide for this contingency. It seems an abstruse and useless *tour de force* to write an extended piece of music which sounds equally well right way up or upside down. In the fifteenth and sixteenth centuries composers, more especially of Flemish schools, notoriously spent immense energy on even more abstruse problems of the kind, and undoubtedly often indulged in their ingenuity for its own sake; but the ingenuity of Bach's invertible fugues is not indulged in for its own sake. It is indulged in because he discovered that totally invertible counterpoint in three or four parts was a thing that might be needed in any triple fugue, and that it could not be produced by accident.

Bach did not, as some people suppose, develop his contrapuntal skill early in life. In spite of his growing tendency to a crystalline clearness in every aspect of his art-forms, he learned neither by *a priori* theory nor by classical precedent, but by trial and error. Although his copies of the works of other composers, ancient and contemporary, fill a considerable bulk in the mass of his autographs, he did not learn anything like as much by classical precedent as he added almost automatically even in the act of copying. His precedents are, in fact, not classical, but archaic; and it was he who developed what could be learned from them into forms that we accept as classical.

Counterpoint is of all musical subjects that in which the confusion between technique and aesthetics shows itself in the most childish forms, both in criticism and in composition. We shall do well to beware of the assertion that any contrapuntal combination is ingenious. Nobody can judge of its ingenuity except people who could have produced it. In the fourteenth century polyphony was being hammered into shape by a process beginning with the more or less reckless use of ornaments in several voices simultaneously proceeding on a foundation of bare fifths, fourths, and octaves. The original conception of harmony was that of doubling a melody in perfect concords. The addition of ornaments produced imperfect chords and discords, which were acceptable in as far as the ornaments glided smoothly and the discords did not dwell on accented moments. Experiments became bolder; and sometimes a drastic leap forwards was made by *quodlibets*, compositions in which several pre-existing tunes were sung together under the order *Marche ou je t'assomme*, and the more intolerable corners were roughly knocked off. This venerable conception survives at the present day, except that we find no corners so intolerable as to be worth knocking off. I would have said, not that it survives, but that it had been recently revived; only the apostolic succession of steam-roller contrapuntists happens to have been preserved by Wagner in the famous combination of three themes in his *Meistersinger* Prelude. Moreover, it has been preserved, at all events in England, by a plausible definition of counterpoint propounded by an Oxford professor, Sir Frederick Gore Ouseley, who stated that counterpoint is the art of combining melodies. Here the word 'art' begs the question. There is obviously no art in allowing Sir Toby Belch, Sir Andrew Aguecheek, and the Clown to sing anything they like in complete independence of each other. The true definition of classical counterpoint is that it is the art of conveying a mass of harmony in a combination of good melodies—that is to say, in a combination of melodies that need no extra notes to make the harmonic sense complete. The discipline by which this art is attained will naturally consist of exercise in problems both more restricted and more extended than any that need appear in free works of art. It has been said of Palestrina, and of other composers earlier and later, as it has been said of great billiard-players, that he makes the notes or the balls go where he wants instead of having to follow their track like ordinary mortals. Rockstro compared Palestrina with earlier great masters such as Josquin des Prés, in that, while Josquin could place a beautiful chord at every turn, Palestrina's proved to have placed themselves in the course of some beautiful contrapuntal imitation. Not only does this ascribe to Palestrina what should be a normal quality of good counterpoint and beautiful harmony, but it actually runs counter to the fact that, while Josquin's contrapuntal devices are present in crystalline clearness, like Bach's two centuries later, Palestrina in his ripest style has removed most of the direct evidence that a definite contrapuntal structure ever existed in his mind.

We are not to infer from this that the highest art is to conceal art. With all respect to Horace, and to the not less venerable authorities who quote him, that represents a childish view both of aesthetics and of technique; and in Great Britain, which, of all countries, is that in which amateurishness is a most dangerous affectation, it amounts in practice to a belief that the highest art is to avoid art. The art by which a composer learns to make the notes go where he wants them is one that is most easily and quickly learned by practice in canonic forms, for these forms compel us to find a possible harmonic meaning for combinations that we would not have invented for ourselves. They are like complicated rhyme-formulas, which often have a deep motive in the structure of the language far more cogent than any desire of ingenuity for its own sake. Thus, for instance, *terza rima* is a *tour de force* in English poetry, where an immense variety of rhymes is available and many rhyming syllables have individual meanings; but *terza rima* is almost forced upon Dante by a language in which rhyme is not only unavoidable, but consists almost wholly in grammatical terminations common to all verbs, nouns, and adjectives, so that the rhyme has no meaning in itself but needs an inherently interesting pattern to make it endurable throughout a long poem. There is no rule whatever by which we can say *a priori* that a contrapuntal device is justified by its ingenuity. The student who excuses a harsh harmony or a grammatical licence by the necessity of a canon must be told that neither the licence nor the canon is necessary. In no case does a contrapuntal device deserve to be called ingenious if the result

31

is ugly, but in the case of a beautiful piece of counterpoint it is equally untrue to say that it is beautiful in spite of its ingenuity. Unquestionably it is ingenious if the beauty could have been obtained by no other means; and this is the case with most of the beautiful contrapuntal devices. Their harmony will prove to be unproducible by other means. How the composer arrived at such a result is no business of ours. By the time he has the enormous experience by which Mozart, Bach, and Brahms produced their mature works, much of it may seem to him to be a matter of luck—that is to say, he will not have thought of every contrapuntal possibility before he actually produced it, and will certainly not go through a process of first putting independent melodies together and then knocking off the intolerable roughnesses; but the luck which serves his purpose does not occur to inexperienced and unpractised artists.

It may be as well now to give some actual illustrations of this matter of counterpoint. First let us begin with the famous case of the *Meistersinger* combination. At the time when Wagner was a subject of controversy—we can afford to ignore recent attempts to belittle him—the anti-Wagnerians found in that combination plenty of occasion to blaspheme. Wagnerians in Grove's *Dictionary* and elsewhere said: 'Who can deny the title of contrapuntist to the composer who achieved this combination of melodies?' People who knew what counterpoint ought to be could deny it loudly and emphatically. The harmony made by this combination of melodies is miserable. All is well so long as the themes are all on one chord, although that chord is poorly and harshly repre-

The Song.

The Guild Banner.

The Master-Singers.

&c.

&c.

&c.

sented, with uncomfortable emphasis on a bare fourth; but in the third bar two of the melodies go crassly into unison or octaves, and in the fourth bar the one accented note of the *Preislied* that should be a sensitive appoggiatura, if it means anything, is doubled, and one can only say fouled, by a flourish in the Apprentices' theme. It has been pointed out to me that, if this combination of melodies is all that matters, it is almost a pity that Wagner did not add a very fine fourth melody, the Toreador's song in *Carmen*, which by no connivance of his own can be added for no less than six bars at the top without making matters any worse. This closes the anti-Wagnerian case. For most of us a sufficient reply is the triumphant fact that the passage as a whole, properly played, sounds magnificent and perfectly smooth. But as the mere combination of melodies sounds nothing of the kind, it is evident that, if Wagner is a great contrapuntist, his genuine counterpoint must lie elsewhere; and as a matter of fact, the combination is held together by some classically perfect counterpoint to which nobody pays any attention.

Let me illustrate in detail how the points which I have censured are absorbed into chromatic harmony of classical beauty and naturalness, how the hideous fourth that aggravates the pair of octaves in the third bar turns out to be part of a progression of interesting chords with the top part moving in smooth contrary motion with the bass, and how the sensitive appoggiatura of the *Preislied* turns out to be an essential part of quite a different chord, well able to bear doubling at the moment of its occurrence, and becomes something equally important but quite different by means of the very flourish in the Apprentices' theme which seemed merely to foul it when we had only the bare combination before us.

Wagner evidently never supposed that his combination of melodies could make counterpoint by itself. The melodies had, in fact, been conceived independently; and the art which combines them lies in the unobtrusive accompaniment. Wagner promptly proceeds to demonstrate this; because after the first four bars he is obliged to keep his counterpoint in play, but has no longer to force a rigid pre-existing material into combination, and there is far less crudity in the whole tangle that develops in complex liveliness for the next twenty bars. Every suspicion of awkwardness is explained away by unobtrusive harmonies, but the occasions for such explanation are few and momentary, and the explanatory harmonies are produced mainly by sustaining notes already present in the themes; which almost proves that the combination tends to explain itself.

The motive for the ostentatious roughness that is the fashion in the most modern counterpoint comes from the fact that classical counterpoint actually attracts no attention. The *Meistersinger* combination itself is already a case that, apart from its accompanying harmonic explanation, may be described as 'stage' counterpoint. It might be argued that there ought to be a certain awkwardness in the fitting of the melodies if they are to be heard as independent things, and the modern composer scornfully rejects the scrupulous art by which Wagner's classical harmony smooths out the primitive roughness of the ostensible counterpoint. Many errors of criticism consist in confusing methods with results. When a critic suspects a composer of pedantic ingenuity, he is apt to tell us that counterpoint is only a means to an end. This is not true. Counterpoint is the art by which a combination of good melodic lines produces complete harmony without the need of any inferior accessory matter. It is ridiculous to say that such art is only a means and not an end in itself. If the counterpoint, with or without accessory matter, is not beautiful, why complain that it is too ingenious? It is not ingenious at all.

Another *a priori* objection must be mentioned, in order to be dismissed as thoroughly unsound in form. We are told that it is psychologically impossible to attend to many things at once. In fact, the psychologists tell us as a scientific fact that nobody can attend to more than two. This is quite true, but it has no effect whatever in limiting the complexities admissible in polyphonic music. No psychologist denies that you cannot hear any number of things at once. He denies only that you attend to more than two; but for my own part I seriously doubt whether in listening to polyphonic music I attend to more than one thing, and that is the total impression. From moment to moment I may notice an effect produced by this or that inner or outer part, but my enjoyment would be a sadly strenuous and uncomfortable affair if I made any conscientious effort to identify in a single hearing all the details which prove that the harmony and form are alive.

If a painter or sculptor shows a consummate knowledge of anatomy, this does not mean that a staff of X-ray experts can reveal actual bones and muscles in the interior of works of art. Nor does it mean that the artist could be entrusted with a surgical operation. It means that his figures present to the eye of the man of science as well as to the eye of the layman the appearance of living figures and not of sacks stuffed with straw or flock. The total impression of good counterpoint is good harmony.

I will conclude with a few classical examples. Triple counterpoint is harmony made by a combination of melodies so contrived that any of them can be a bass to the others. The necessity for its existence is evident in an art-form like that of fugue; for, if any of the melodies is not capable of making a good bass to the others, the bass will be deprived of its fair share of the themes. The question whether the listener can attend to all three at once does not arise. He can recognize the whole combination, and he can enjoy the unity in variety which results from presenting the same harmonic and melodic elements in six different positions. As a matter of fact, in Bach's standard type of triple counterpoint the three themes are remarkably transparent to each other. Psychologists may say that you cannot attend to all three: but you certainly cannot only attend to the combination as a single impression, while you can detect at any moment the elements of contrast between the three members. There is usually one theme that skips energetically, another that trickles smoothly, and a third which completes and enriches the whole harmony with a slow chain of suspensions. Bach attained maturity in the art of combining different melodies much sooner than he attained it in stretti or combinations of a theme with itself. I cannot think of any crude examples of double, triple, and quadruple counterpoint in Bach's works; but there are early works in which he treated a single theme awkwardly. Opinions will differ where the line should be drawn. In my opinion Busoni draws it for Bach with a fastidiousness which he certainly does not apply to his own compositions: rejecting, for example, the D major fugue in the second book of *Das Wohltemperirte Klavier*, a stretto fugue which I shall always maintain to be magnificent. For my own part, I put decidedly outside the pale the famous fugues in D sharp minor and A minor in the first book. When I am told that these are learned and ingenious I dispute the learning and ingenuity of their admirers.

A common prejudice, unworthy of grown-up persons, assumes that of two kinds of technical problem whichever is studied later is the more difficult. This mistake is quite common in the schedules of examinations in playing. On the pianoforte scales in thirds are naturally studied later than plain scales; and a piece that contains a scale in thirds is without further inquiry graded as more difficult than a piece which does not. I once encountered an exalted person who played the violin—it were indiscreet to ask how—and he was convinced that Beethoven's Violin Concerto was easy, because at no moment does it contain a scheduled *tour de force*. Belief in this naïve criterion is very harmful in the education of players. In the technique of composition it is too ridiculous to do much harm, and the nonsense that it produces in analysis and criticism is too perishable to matter.

When we are told in the preface to an excellent miniature score of Mendelssohn's *Elijah* that the Overture deals with some of the more difficult contrapuntal problems, such as treatment by inversion, the *naïveté* calls for comment, because, incredible as it may seem, it represents a belief seriously held by some teachers. Any theme will invert. All that you need do is to write it upside down. You need not even write it. If you hold the theme upside down, it will be inverted and turned backwards as well; and if you do not wish it to be thus also what the learned in such matters call *cancrizans*, you must hold it before a looking-glass to get it reflected in the right direction.

If the inversion is ugly, why does the composer use it? The only art in the use of an inversion is the choice of themes and positions of which the inversion happens to be good. A composer who works habitually at contrapuntal forms is likely to conceive a large number of themes that will invert well. This sets up a habit of mind that is favourable to the invention of such themes. It does not set up a skill in tinkering preconceived ideas until they will invert. If a theme needs tinkering before it will invert, the composer will simply not invert it. Purcell's themes will invert more often than not; Brahms's almost as often as Purcell's; Beethoven's seldom, and then in compositions avowedly fugal.

Now the D sharp minor and A minor fugues in the first book of the Forty-Eight have themes which Bach treats by inversion, though the inversions are definitely ugly. The inversion of the D sharp minor theme produces a feeble tautology not evident in the original. The inversion of the A minor theme begins well, but risks lockjaw when the downward plunge which was originally its best feature becomes like the upwards force of a dentist's gag.

Both fugues exhaust, I hope, the possibilities of stretto; but the stretti do not make beautiful harmony. They narrowly achieve grammatic sense. The composer's material is not naturally giving rise to these forms. The forms are forced upon it from outside, and noble musical rhetoric asserts itself with evident relief when the devices are abandoned.

There is something almost uncanny in the difference between such exercises and the masterpieces where the matter produces the form. I wish I had time to vindicate the D major fugue in the second book, which Busoni rejects, and also to discriminate between the elements of pure art and of technical exercise in *Die Kunst der Fuge*, which at its worst contains nothing like the crudeness of the D sharp minor and A minor fugues; but I end this lecture by directing special attention to the great B flat minor from the second book of the Forty-Eight. I choose this in preference to the more famous and equally noble B flat minor from the first book, just because it is a schematic composition of which a superficial description might lead one to suspect it of being an exercise.

The points which illustrate my arguments are: first, that the inversions of the theme and of its counter-subject, singly and in combination, are not less beautiful than the originals; secondly, that the stretti all make beautiful harmony without the slightest effort; thirdly, that, instead of abandoning the ingenuities in order to make a purely musical climax, Bach achieves his highest rhetoric by the closest combination of all. (This, by the way, is also the case in the D major fugue which Busoni dislikes.) But there is another point, which lies outside the composition, and which shows what happens when material and form are true functions of each other. I have expressed the hope that in the A minor and D sharp minor fugues Bach had exhausted the possible combinations. He had, in fact, done more, since he included several that he would later have thought impossible; but he could have designed at least eight other fugues with the subject and scheme of this B flat minor fugue. And probably these would not have exhausted the combinations. He has taken the closest stretti, those in which the answer follows the subject at the second note and at the interval of a seventh; but there is another set of stretti at two beats and an octave, and a third set at a whole bar and a ninth. And in the present set of stretti Bach has used only a quarter of the combinations where the direct theme and its inversion answer each other.

LECTURE III

PERFECT integrity in a work of art implies that all it needs for its explanation is to be found within it. We have already seen a few of the more obvious illustrations of this in showing that technical problems are essentially aesthetic problems, which concern every lover of the art, and not professional or trade secrets.

To the non-musician it may seem hopeless to maintain the paradox that there is nothing in purely instrumental music that does not explain itself, and most musicians are apt to be equally sceptical in this matter. Nevertheless, I hope to show that the experience which makes a piece of music enjoyable is an experience accessible to all, and that no technical knowledge is relevant to it except that which enables us to become more quickly familiar with the music. Although art exists and must be judged only in individual works, the experience necessary for enjoying each work cannot be confined to that work. And we must not forbid, though we must severely control, the influence of many human experiences, general and artistic, on our enjoyment of the single work. Poetry uses human speech. You cannot learn a language from a single poem, and the most rigorously abstract of modern poets cannot even enjoy their meaningless word-patterns unless in daily life they still understand language normally enough to recognize nonsense when they see or hear it.

If any work of art could explain itself to an experience confined to its own materials, a musical composition might be able to do so; and music and architecture certainly make themselves understood more universally and with less appeal to outside experience than any other arts. We have lost our simple Victorian faith in the universal intelligibility of classical music. In the seventies Macfarren, though he suffered from the most naïve readiness to interpret medieval music by nineteenth-century habits, had the wisdom to point out that the cultivated Chinaman finds European music as unintelligible as we find Chinese music. Neither Macfarren nor all but few, if any, of modern European orientalists and musical folk-lorists can be trusted to keep their interpretations of oriental and ancient music free from unconscious confusion with ideas of their own civilization. Hannibal crossed the Alps with the utmost expedition, but the schoolboy who translated *summa diligentia* by 'on the top of a diligence' was less confused in his notions than the learned writer who tells us in one of our chief works of reference that we need not expect to find written records of so simple a procedure as singing in thirds.

I shall not attempt to deal, here or at any other time, with any music but the classics of our own Western civilization. Two cardinal errors are to be avoided, both in dealing with these classics and their merits and in comparing them with alien systems. The first error I have just mentioned. Macfarren avoided it in as far as he recognized that music cannot be said to be universally intelligible, but he constantly fell into it whenever he tried to describe any music that he could not conceive as written by himself.

43

This is a natural, and not always unamiable, error. Dame Ethel Smyth has quoted as a perfect example of psychological blindness the case of a friend who said: 'I consider that I understand a person when, if I were to be in the same position as that person, I should act in the same way'. It is impossible to frame a more accurate illustration of a person whose point of view is exclusively self-centred. But Mac-farren's very efforts to attain a detached point of view betrayed him constantly into the opposite error, which is perhaps more serious. The self-centred person may not know himself as thoroughly as the oracle required, but at all events he does not disbelieve in his own existence, and a broad-minded view on ancient and oriental music is easily affected by persons who are really only substituting a profound scepticism about music of all kinds. In a famous passage more valuable as prose than as a contribution to musical thought, Cardinal Newman has expressed a not uncommon doubt whether our music is not after all a game rather than an art with foundations in truth. Now, those of us who have no time to study oriental and ancient music may be pardoned for suspecting that arts so remote from their comprehension may be arbitrary games; but for European musicians who devote their lives to the study of our musical classics of the last five hundred years there is no excuse for such an attitude. If they are wrong they have failed to understand the essentials of music; if they are right they expose themselves to the condemnation of Herbert Spencer, who on playing a friendly game of billiards with a stranger put away his cue when the stranger made a break of sixty and said that the attainment of such preposterous skill in a mere game was proof of a mis-spent life.

There is a difference between a work of art and a chess problem. Problems have been called the 'poetry of chess', a proposition often hotly disputed by chess-players. They certainly are selections of the elements of chess arranged on highly artificial principles with the utmost regard for economy and several other qualities of high aesthetic value. Still, it cannot be claimed that the materials of chess, whether in play or problem, have any power to explain themselves without instruction in the rules of the game. Capablanca tells us that at a very early age, without any lessons in chess, he had by merely watching his father and his uncle at play discovered that his uncle moved a knight incorrectly; but the observant eye of the *enfant terrible* is not restricted to so narrow a field of observation, and we might study the shapes of chessmen till Doomsday before we could discover any necessary connexion between them and their correct moves.

Musical theory has been wrecked again and again by efforts to base it upon natural acoustic principles. The attempt is vain, as are all attempts to reduce art to science. In as far as theories of harmony go beyond empiric observation of the practice of great masters, they tend towards uncontrollable pseudo-scientific speculations. And I frankly have more faith in your patience to listen to the discussion of such things than I have in my own patience to discuss them; but I have no doubt that the coherence of musical works of art rests on principles more universal and more self-explanatory than the laws of chess. Nor am I deterred from asserting this belief by the fact that some of the most essential elements of music cannot possibly be described except in technical terms. This does not mean that they are professional matters. Why should it mean anything of the kind?

Let me devote the rest of this lecture to an illustration of the most technical subject in all music: the subject on which text-books are inadequate and on which many questions which still survive in examinations show not the slightest sign of intelligence. Before I terrify any of you by naming the subject, I will ask you: first, whether the taste of a peach can be appreciated by any but a connoisseur? and secondly, whether connoisseurship in peaches carries with it any capacity to describe the taste of a peach in terms that will convey an idea of it to a person who has never had the experience? If your reply to these questions is that this is a profound professional matter and a field for connoisseurship not less exalted than that of wine, I shall then be prepared to believe that tonality is a profound professional matter of which the sense is inaccessible to any but professional musicians. The taste of venison is not an everyday experience for all people, and those to whom it is new, even when they are so highly professional as cooks, have been known, when not forewarned, to assume that the haunch of venison is some more familiar joint that has been kept too long. Doubts aesthetically analogous were cast upon Wagner's tonality by anti-Wagnerians. The extension of the word 'taste' over all the five senses has been very useful to critics and connoisseurs, especially in the light of the Latin proverb, which firmly removes it from

46

the sphere of a dispute. Tonality is a thing which you can no more describe except by metaphors and comparisons than you can describe the taste of a peach, or the precise difference between venison and mutton or beef that has been kept too long.

The nearest parallel to tonality that I can find in other arts or senses is perspective. I have, both in lectures and in writings, carefully worked out the objections and limits to this analogy. The shortest working-out would take at least twenty minutes to deliver, and I am tired of the comments of critics who skip my explanations and assail me with the very objections which these explanations have discussed; so please believe that I know and have considered all that can be said against the parallel between tonality and perspective. The objections are not more serious than those which can be raised to the statement that 'scarlet is like the sound of a trumpet', the famous remark made by a man who, having been blind from birth, received sight by means of an operation.

A picture that is in correct perspective represents three dimensions on a flat surface by faithfully obeying the laws of optics within the limits of single-eye vision. If in a picture gallery you shut one eye, the perspective of most of the pictures will seem far more realistic. What has really happened is that by shutting one eye you make the walls and frames appear flat, only you ignore that appearance, and therefore the flat picture is at no disadvantage. The correctness of the perspective depends upon the painter's having referred all the objects in his picture to one horizon; or, conversely, to his having painted the

47

picture from one point of view, the point of view being that of the spectator and the vanishing-point of all lines being within the picture in the middle of its horizon.

A musical composition in classical tonality has a tonic chord, which will normally be the final chord of the whole, and round which all other chords will be grouped in definite relation. Before the art of harmony was developed this tonic sense asserted itself in melody, though not always in ways that lend themselves to our harmonic interpretations. The non-musician who is accustomed to as much music as assaults his ears from the common barrel-organ is by no means without a sense of classical tonality. It may be a very bad sense, but it is no more primitive than a diet of tripe and onions. Few people can be so stone-deaf as not to realize when they hear it that a chord of the subdominant will not fit the sixth bar of our National Anthem; and if there is anyone who does not recognize something wrong there I will not inquire further into his capacity to enjoy music.

In what has been called the Golden Age of music, the age of pure vocal polyphony that became a great art in the fifteenth century and reached its perfect maturity at the end of the sixteenth, there was no need for tonality to be constantly asserting the kind of harmonic perspective analogous to that of a picture with no vestiges of primitive technique. There are plenty of beautiful pictures that imply a different horizon for each item that can be viewed separately; and, while we label the masters of such art primitive, we have outgrown the philistinism that prefers con-

48

sistent perspective to all decorative merits, and we have learned humility in our criticisms of Chinese and Japanese art which, as Macaulay would have put it, violates every rule of perspective.

In the eighteen-forties an editor of the Musical Antiquarian Society acquired merit by publishing a volume of motets by William Byrd. Perhaps he acquired the more merit since he disapproved of them strongly, and expressed his opinions honestly in a preface in which, while deprecating the judgement of Byrd's contemporaries that they were 'angellical and divine', he grudgingly conceded that, in spite of certain monstrous false relations, they were as good as could be expected of a composer who was shackled by the Church modes, in illustration of which he quoted one of the most wonderful passages in all sixteenth-century music, the opening of Palestrina's *Stabat Mater*, as a curious instance of the uncertainty regarding the scale prevalent in the time of the author.

A favourite examination question of mine is this: 'Quote from memory, or invent, some progression characteristic of the Elizabethan period.' One of the answers I got was the opening of 'O who will o'er the downs so free?' If the Palestrina example has the perspective of a Chinese painting, my candidate's example has the painted relief of letters in a trade sign. I am afraid that the Victorian editor of the Musical Antiquarian Society would have thought this an advance upon Palestrina's tonality. As a matter of fact, in all the large-scale uses of tonality the exponents of the unrevised *Hymns Ancient and Modern* style were crassly ignorant; and the statements and rules about tonality that survive to this day in text-books are as misleading as the phlogiston theory of chemistry. Unfortunately, the large-scale facts of tonality would need the whole of the present course of lectures to present even in outline. I once rashly undertook to demonstrate for my Edinburgh classes the balance of keys in a single Mozart rondo; and I found that the demonstration of that one piece occupied three lectures. Perhaps I may risk merely mentioning what I undertook to demonstrate.

The subject was the finale of Mozart's Trio for Piano, Clarinet, and Viola. The demonstration took for granted how the home tonic was defined, and ignored all possibility of any more primitive and less rigid earlier and later systems of tonality. It undertook to show that as soon as the key-centre was changed the original tonic chord no longer suggested the tonic, but quite unequivocally took its proper place in the new key. It showed that, nevertheless, if the new key was not too remote, a return could be made to the home tonic without any feeling that the bounds of a single flow of melody had been exceeded.

The first change of key in an actively disposed composition in the major mode will normally be to the dominant. Within the original key the chord on the dominant is penultimate in every normal cadence. When this chord has become a key-centre in its own right, the home-tonic chord becomes its subdominant, and retains no vestige of its original tonic sense. This and all other facts I demonstrated by showing the effect of a return to the main theme in the tonic at each point where the local sequence of chords would permit if we knew nothing of the larger context. It soon became evident that quite a long stay in the key of the dominant was powerless to convey a sense that the music had travelled beyond the bounds of an extended lyric melody, and that the home tonic would not sink below the horizon until some stress had been laid upon the dominant of the dominant. For this I have found it necessary to coin the term 'enhanced dominant'. And it is a shocking evidence of the incompetence of much widely accepted teaching that there are few, if any, commentaries that can be trusted not to treat an enhanced dominant as a key in its own right.

The rondo of Mozart's Clarinet Trio is almost an encyclopedia of the facts of simple key-relations, which it demonstrates all the more impressively because the whole composition is ostentatiously unintellectual and devoted to pleasure in the alternation of simple melodies. If we appreciate the Greek accuracy and subtlety of its key-relations, and their connexion with its thematic structure, we shall find grim satisfaction, such as Tertullian ascribes to the angels who rejoice to contemplate the torments of the damned, in our superiority to the childish critics who tell us that this movement is an unimportant and lazy piece of work. I regret that I cannot illustrate it further, or give you the very convincing demonstrations of what will happen if we substitute one thing for another, or return to our tonic at the wrong moment, or shorten any of the passages which delay Mozart's return until the right moment. I can only tell you that his final stroke is to repeat as the triumphant end of the whole composition a passage which had earlier been heard at the very same pitch as being on the dominant of the key of the subdominant. Some of our bright young men, or dull old men, sneer at the two pages of leisurely epilogue that precedes this close, and that has thematically no more connexion with the rest of the movement than the other passages have with each other; but if you leave it out or shorten it the close of the movement will be disastrously suggestive of a return to the subdominant, and if the two pages of epilogue had more connexion with the other themes the style of the whole movement would have been stultified.

I shall have more to say about tonality in later lectures. The harmony of classical music from Haydn to Beethoven is far less elaborate in detail than that of Bach. And commentators have been known to remark that no great composer has contributed less to the progress of harmony than Beethoven. Such a remark can be made only by a critic who has never regarded the facts of harmony on a large scale at all; and to this day harmony books, even of a most advanced kind, never seem to take a longer view than some half-dozen chords at a time. The harmony of the dramatic sonata-style of Haydn, Mozart, and Beethoven is in detail simpler than that of Bach, because you cannot build large-scale relations of key on a basis of elaborate harmonic detail, any more than you can construct a dramatically exciting play out of epigrams. Beethoven's harmony may become as abstruse as the profoundest of Bach's figured chorales if his task allows him to devote a short section of a work to matters of local harmonic interest, as in the *Variations on a Waltz of Diabelli*.

Large-scale harmony once more became abstruse when Wagner, anticipated in detail by Chopin and Liszt, developed the art of so accentuating an ornamental note in one key that it conveyed a sense of some vastly remote key. If the extended use of such an art is not to degenerate into nonsense, the composer's sense of large-scale tonality must be very powerful, and he must be able to convey it to the listener. The permanently astounding paradoxes of the *Tristan* Prelude are not more characteristic of Wagner than the opening of *Das Rheingold* with its several minutes of one single chord, or the opening of *Die Walküre* in sequences which take sixteen bars to move one step up the scale of D minor.

I have not time to deal with more modern developments of harmony, and any attempt to do so will involve me in controversies more interesting humanly for the acrimony which they may develop than musically for the enlightenment they may give. I will only say that one thing is unquestionably missing in most of our new harmonic experiments: and that is, evidence that they are helpful to the development of music on a large scale. When a tendency in recent harmony is definite enough to be the subject of propaganda, the propagandists still seem to concern themselves with six bars at a time at the utmost. Atonality and polytonality are severe discipline. I feel sceptical about their independence and novelty, especially when I find that a violinist who has great difficulty in finding the correct intonation of a thread in a polytonal composition can play it with ease if I support it on the commonplace and slightly oily Spohr-like harmonies which I suspect to have been lurking at the back of the composer's mind. Not so can the harmonic profundities of Wagner be made to vanish.

LECTURE IV

WE have now to consider some paradoxes that are far more deeply involved in the integrity of works of art than any questions of the influence of one kind of art upon another. The vexed questions of programme music, and of conflict between the claims of musical form and the treatment of words in vocal music, and the endless possibilities of confusion and imperfection in the art of opera, are all easy and trivial matters compared with the dangers that arise from confusing processes with results. This confusion is not the same as that which confuses means with ends. The ingenious work of art is often criticized for sacrificing means to ends by critics whose views are not sound as to how far things that happen to be means are worthy to be regarded as ends in themselves; and in any case we are inclined greatly to overrate the practical danger of such a confusion. The golfer's end is the hole, and he must know its direction and be able, like any other marksman, to allow for the force of the wind; but his duty is to keep his eye on the ball. It is a brutal truth that in music, as in all the arts, most composers produce their worst work in the avowed pursuit of lofty ideals, and there are abundant classical examples of great works produced, not only with an avowedly technical aim, but even with an appeal for immediate popularity.

The question now before us is this: every work of art being produced under stress of practical necessities without which it could not have existed, how far do these necessities remain in the finished result in such a form that we must know them in order to enjoy the work? If there is any such thing as perfection and integrity in art, the only possible answer to this question is that, to use an inelegant metaphor, what the finished result cannot digest must be ignored or regarded as outside it. The historian must not confuse between his estimate of the historical influence of a work and the permanent value of the work in itself. The student of technique must neither be too ready to dismiss means from the category of ends, nor to confuse the way in which a thing is done with what is done. Smooth harmony can be achieved by avoiding consecutive fifths and octaves, by resolving all discords immediately downwards by step and all leading notes upwards by step, and by avoiding progressions that are ambiguous in tonality, especially those that follow the dominant by the subdominant in such a way as to draw attention to the tritone fourth. But this is not even a technical definition of smooth harmony. The observance of these rules does not even amount to 'safety first', though there are exercises in which these rules will enable a beginner to express the musical equivalent of 'a cat sat on a mat'.

Unfortunately, a great deal of quite advanced training is often devoted to inculcating the notion that the more closely a style obeys such rules the purer it will be. For instance, the rule against consecutive fifths is very stringent in pure polyphony, and there are conditions in which Beethoven and Wagner, sometimes even Strauss, will show themselves extremely scrupulous to observe it. As a teacher I find myself all in favour of enforcing it upon students with a strictness which most examiners will to-day consider old-fashioned and pedantic; but such broad-minded people are in revolt against a doctrine current in my youth, which inculcated that the more nearly you approach to a pair of consecutive fifths the less smooth is your style. Now there is no period of history or phase of musical education in which such a view ought ever to have been orthodox.

Time fails to work out the very difficult arguments that arise from this rule, but it is possible to show the conclusion of the whole matter in two illustrations. The object of training students in exercises where the rule is enforced under difficulties is to develop in them an ear sensitive enough to such matters to appreciate genuine refinements of musical style when they hear them, and eventually to be able to achieve such a style themselves.

In a composition called a *moresca* or *frottola*, Orlando di Lasso has written a certain progression of chords to the text *miaow, miaow*. The progression breaks the most elementary rule of counterpoint or harmony and is utterly inadmissible in pure polyphony. If you find any trace of it in Palestrina you have to deal with a misprint or a slip of the pen. Orlando di Lasso is quite as great a master of polyphony as Palestrina, and has a very much wider range of style, being not only a writer of great motets and not much less great masses, but perhaps the most prolific sixteenth-century musical illustrator of every kind of secular poetry, French, German, Italian, and Latin. Traces of such a progression are as non-existent in a motet or madrigal by Lasso as in the works of Palestrina; but Lasso did write this progression as part of a coherent, if naughty, scheme. In the aesthetic system of Debussy they would be perfectly proper, because his system is in many respects the reverse of that of classical polyphony, or of any kind of polyphony; and as such it has a purity of its own which he maintains with the scrupulousness of antiseptic surgery. There is room in musical aesthetics for the most opposite doctrines, but there is no room whatever for the doctrine that you must keep away from the risk of a direct collision of consecutive fifths.

The mature, broad-minded view is that such things may be done if one of the peccant notes is *only* a passing note. Captain Marryat with his bluff humanity persuaded even the mid-Victorian circulating libraries and British parents to accept a view at once severe and humane of the inadmissibility of the word 'only'. I refer to the case of the poor little nurse who had been in trouble, but who for that very reason was a suitable nurse if the guardians of the baby who was in need of her could only be persuaded to overlook the fact that she had had no right to have a baby of her own. They were not satisfied with her excuse that it was 'only a little one'. You may take it that when a licence is found in a great style, the excuse for it will never prove to be that the peccant element is *only* this or that. The explanation will always turn out to involve a wide context, and to be something by no means to be ignored, but, on the contrary, to be regarded as highly important.

There is a wonderful Amen of Palestrina, so wonderful that you may listen to it for years without adding to your quiet satisfaction in it the discovery that it is unusual. Its harmony is perfectly pure, but seven pairs of consecutive fifths and octaves are avoided only by a crotchet which is not even a passing note, but is part of the prevalent concords. Of course, it is evident that this crotchet is part of a theme, a fact which makes it easy to recognize; but few vaulted buildings, such as are generally favourable for the sound of Palestrina's choral writing, are so free from confusion in their reverberations that any listener can count upon always distinguishing this very essential note. Now the broad-minded examiner will think me pedantic for blue-pencilling such a progression as this in an answer to an examination question. But I cannot accept the excuse that the fifths are produced by something which is only a passing note. That presupposes that we do not notice that the passing note is a fifth. The most old-fashioned examiner would object if we magnified the passage until this fifth evidently made a chord. Tempo is one of the vital elements in all harmony, and I am far from maintaining that the passage thus magnified is the same as the passage at a quick flow; but I do stoutly maintain that even naïve listeners—I mean listeners uncorrupted by professional information—should be credited with the ability to develop ears highly sensitive to the most delicate meanings of melody and harmony, and that to this end all musical students should be trained to recognize harmonic meanings in rapid details—in other words, that their exercises should be in a harmony that bears magnifying. And it is quite certain that you cannot have it both ways. This progression does not bear magnifying and if you are content habitually to dismiss the passing note as only a passing note, how is it that you can claim to appreciate the beauty of Palestrina's *Amen*?

Most of the confusion that is set up in the minds both of students and of teachers on this subject comes from the natural tendency when correcting an exercise to recognize each mistake with an agonized intake of the breath and with other symptoms of imminent lockjaw. It is true, as I have pointed out before, that Professor Higgins and Eliza Doolittle needed to devote unremitting attention to the utmost refinements that phonograph records could show in distinguishing between innumerable sounds of human speech before she could control her utterance well enough to pass as a person fit to present at a Royal garden party. It is equally true that she passed through an intermediate stage in which every syllable was enunciated in a voice of beautiful quality and accurate intonation, while the substance of what she said produced the greatest shock that the modern stage has received since the box on the ear which devastated the French theatre in the time of Molière. The moral of which is that the musical student needs more protection from debilitating and unsound technical precautions than from any risks of making his own mistakes.

The doctrine that not only fifths, but the remote risk of fifths, must be avoided has not, I think, been officially avowed, but a statement arising from the same assumption has often been current from classical times onwards, with results not less disastrous because it asserts a fact, though it gives the wrong reason for it. We are told that the severity of rules for two-part and three-part harmony becomes relaxed as the difficulty of observing them increases with the number of parts. A student who has been taught this has practically been told that he need never trouble to acquire a good technique. I was told by a pupil of Liszt that one of his proverbs was: 'There is no mercy in art'.

The student of two-part and three-part harmony is confronted with a large number of vexatious rules. Most of these are necessary because with two or three parts it is difficult to produce rich and full harmony. Such rules automatically cease to have any meaning in harmony of more parts, where the difficulty is rather to be clear and to prevent any of the parts from sounding superfluous. Of course, the student really should study two-part and three-part harmony in two widely separated stages. So long as he is handling two and three parts merely because he has not the skill to spell out four or more, his exercises should be elementary; and he should not be kept at them too long, but should proceed betimes to what is a more normal kind of music. The advanced student should then return to the noble economy and the lean athletic styles by which two parts or three parts can be made to sound as rich as eight.

Meantime, all teaching and criticism of musical texture should be designed so as never to confuse between methods and results. The student need not expect to see a direct connexion between such exercises as those of scholastic counterpoint and actual music. For musical criticism and analysis the danger of such a confusion might have existed with sixteenth-century music, but for the fact that the teaching of counterpoint was during the nineteenth century so distorted by feeble attempts to bring it up to date that no accurate observer can possibly suppose that from Cherubini onwards its academically accepted rules refer to any known artistic language.

The general type of confusion between means and ends persists to-day with subjects much more advanced and of popular interest. Few musicians can be trusted to keep their power of appreciating classical orchestration free from contamination with their experience of what is good practical advice for students. If we can see no more in Beethoven's orchestration than was seen by Rimsky-Korsakov, to whom it was nearly as obsolete as a tricycle with solid tyres is to the owner of a Rolls-Royce, then we shall certainly not appreciate, much less achieve, the splendours of Rimsky-Korsakov's brilliant and meticulously pure orchestration; and though we may easily emulate the perky provinciality and pedantry of his mind, we shall suffer in our own estimation from the hopeless disadvantages of being British, whether Northern or Southern, instead of having the privilege of being Russian, and therefore romantic and exotic.

The conclusion of this matter is that, whether in counterpoint or in orchestration, the student must be trained in a meticulous, but genuine, purity of style. At present, much of our academic training is lax where it ought to be severe, and timid where it ought to stimulate the student to be bold; but even the soundest practical training will not protect the critic and lover of music from confusing between methods and results. I have often had occasion to point out by way of illustration that the doctor who asks his patient to say 'ninety-nine' is not pronouncing a magic formula. I do not know how French doctors obtain the requisite resonances from their patients' interiors, but I know that they do not ask them to say 'Quatrevingt-dix-neuf'. Many of the rules and practices which the best training will enforce upon students have the purpose of producing habits and skills quite as remote from the superficial appearance of the exercise. I need not illustrate this subject further, but pass at once to the conclusion that one of the most cramping and inadequate of criteria is that which estimates the value of a work of art according to whether it is a good model for students. Students themselves, if they are allowed to believe this, may perhaps not degenerate on the lines of the don who refused to read Homer for fear of spoiling his grasp of Attic Greek, but they will assuredly develop the perkiness of Rimsky-Korsakov without his genius; and, given opportunity, will do far worse by way of bowdlerizing works of genius than Rimsky-Korsakov did with his friend Moussorgsky's *Boris Godounov*. The confusion between history and aesthetics can be even more disastrous to our capacity to understand music than the confusion arising from methods of training. The historic importance of a work of art is obviously separable from its aesthetic value. *Lilliburlero* jingled a king off his throne, but effected nothing that directly concerns musical history; though it is not merely external politics that are irrelevant to musical values, but many of the most important factors and tendencies in music itself.

My beloved master Parry presents in his numerous and stimulating writings on music abundant instances of the fallacies which arise from confusing history with aesthetics. Between him and the art of Mozart there was an obvious incompatibility of temper, aggravated, no doubt, by the revolt from the curiously ignorant idolatry of Mozart prevalent in his youth: an idolatry which not only consistently selected the more trivial of Mozart's numerous works for its worship, but displayed the utmost reverence for spurious works, like the so-called Twelfth Mass, which ought never to have deceived a competent musician for a moment. We have not yet freed ourselves from the results of this idolatry. Mozart wrote many more than twelve masses, and his genuine Twelfth Mass is a very beautiful, if very unecclesiastical, work which is not included in our English editions of Mozart's Masses. These, however, include the spurious Twelfth Mass and four other forgeries by the same author, all of them as near rubbish as makes no difference; but whether it was or was not possible in Parry's generation for a liberal-minded musician to develop a taste for Mozart, Parry would in any case have suffered from an inveterate and deliberately developed tendency to regard all works of art as leading to something beyond. Mozart and Haydn at their best were for Parry necessary processes leading to Beethoven and destined to be superseded by him.

Now here the doctrine of Art for Art's sake becomes important, and its two cardinal errors may be for the moment left out of account. It errs in spelling Art with a capital A, as if anything existed except individual works of art; and it errs, or at all events is misapplied, by being inculcated as if it were a method instead of a result. I firmly believe that a work of art exists for its own sake, but I might not be able to put up a very strong fight against anyone who should tell me that it was a bad doctrine to put forward as practical advice. In any case, many, if not most, of the great results in art and life have been achieved by aiming at something else; or, at all events, by concentrating on the means as soon as the aim has been determined sufficiently to ensure that we do not fire in a totally wrong direction. Whether you like Mozart or not, you must understand him as if the work you are contemplating existed alone in the world.

This does not mean that you can dispense with a large mass of knowledge which could be presented in an historic form, but it means that that knowledge is of matters inside the work and only accidentally of matters outside it. If you are told that a certain aria in an opera was inserted to please a certain singer, forget it. Either the aria is the right thing in the right place, or it is not. On the other hand, the knowledge that you need in order to perform Mozart in the right style and to understand the style both of the performance and of the composition when you listen is knowledge which is often more easily conveyed in historical than in other terms; but ultimately all that is relevant in such knowledge belongs to the substance of the work, just as, to use a former illustration, ancient views as to the respectability of piracy and the importance of decorous funerals explain themselves with romantic and tragic intensity in the poetry of Homer and Sophocles.

Take again the case of the choral works of Bach. Until quite recent times it was maintained that Bach's orchestration was negligible. We now know by experiment with instruments which, if not Bach's, are capable of playing what he wrote, that under proper conditions Bach's orchestration is part of a normal and mature aesthetic system. Such knowledge is obtained through historic research into the conditions in which Bach's works were performed, but it becomes a set of purely aesthetic principles inherent in the music. And I have often had occasion to point out that some of the historic conditions do not become so absorbed, and might as well never have existed—that, for instance, the authority of Bach himself does not compel us to follow his precedent and flog the ringleaders of the choir after an atrocious performance.

A history of music, like that of all arts, falls into periods of pioneer work, of artistic maturity, of decadence, of revolution, and of renascence. Most writers on music, even when, like Parry, they are great composers, seem impelled by a strong sense of duty to put their reflections into historical form. The disadvantages of this tendency are painfully evident in the paralysis which overtakes them all as soon as they are confronted with mature works, and I cannot see any compensating advantages. We ought all to be grateful to Schweitzer for stating, as far as I know for the first time, the cardinal truth that in music of all arts perfection is essential, and that the works at periods in which it was not attainable are perishable. Far be it from me to suggest that we should allow them to perish. On the contrary, the very historians who are so helpless, so inarticulate, and so dangerously sceptical about great music, become stimulating and interesting when they are dealing with archaic and transitional works. Here, in fact, they are forced, in spite of their historical bias, to make some approach towards considering these works as things in themselves. The doctrine that such and such a composition is wonderful for the time at which it was written represents an insufferably perky and patronizing attitude if it is applied to Palestrina, Byrd, Tallis, Bach, Handel, Haydn, Mozart, and Beethoven. When we advance in the nineteenth century our patronage begins to yield to Macaulay's pride in his own enlightened age.

No mature work of art is wonderful for the time at which it was written. It is simply wonderful at all times. A naïve belief is now prevalent that all great artists have been in advance of their time. The effect of this doctrine is to make the average artist of the present day ready to believe that it is his duty to be unintelligible to his contemporaries. That is not difficult. All he need do is to be unintelligible to himself; but, as a matter of fact, it is not true that all great artists have been in advance of their time; and it is quite certain that the contemporaries of those who were in advance did not recognize the fact, even if the artists themselves did. Bach was obviously, unmistakably, and avowedly, a hundred years behind his time. He differed from his predecessors, as

Schweitzer demonstrates, in the all-important fact that his works were mature and theirs were not. That is one reason why the musical historian is so much happier in dealing with the seventeenth century instead of with the eighteenth. With the seventeenth century he is dealing with everything that led not only to Bach and Handel, but to Mozart and to all later music up to Wagner, and his tendency is to see in pioneer work the prophecy of all the glories together; nor is he necessarily or often guilty of an anachronism in this. The pioneers themselves are often deliberately aiming at what they realized in later art, and the historian is in sympathy with them just because he sees beyond the immaturity of their achievements, though he must, if he has any sense of proportion, judge that immaturity more severely than the pioneer artists could have judged it themselves without inhibiting their efforts altogether.

The danger of all this historical sympathy is manifest in many freaks of modern fashion. We get up archaic works and listen, or think we listen, with rapt attention to music, whereas we are spending, as the pioneer artists themselves no doubt did, a great deal of trouble and money upon stage accessories which are really very much more artistic and mature than the music. You will find in the *Denkmäler der Tonkunst* an opera by Marcantonio Cesti, *Il Pomo d'oro*, written for some royal wedding at Dresden. The learned editor talks of the classical perfection of its choruses in terms that would make you think that great music was in question. I hope that I am not less capable than most musicians of doing my duty to pioneer work, but I frankly own that a fleeting

68

glance at the music is quite enough for me so long as I am not engaged in historical research, and that my entire pleasure in this publication lies in the twenty full-page engravings of the gorgeous scenery in which this otherwise very primitive opera was acted. If anyone should ever go to the expense of producing *Il Pomo d'oro*, I should consider the production an absolute fraud if, failing a reproduction of the actual scenery, a spectacle of the same calibre were not organized, with results which, I regret to say, would make the music an almost negligible feature of the whole.

Far be it from me to deny that in archaic and transitional periods, not excluding decadent periods, music has been produced that has permanent value for its own sake; and I am not prepared to maintain that an absolutely sharp line can on principle be drawn between the composers for whom no historical allowance need be made and those with whom it is necessary to consider the time at which they wrote. But I find myself in thorough agreement with Schweitzer that the distinction is much clearer in music than in other arts. Musicians, however, ought to envy the much wider standards of culture that are enforced upon the directors of picture-galleries, who are responsible for the preservation of many works of art far less important than those which we musicians will condescend to keep alive in our repertoires. Time is less elastic than wall-space, for you cannot hear a piece of music at once, and the years of man are but as threescore and ten. Few practical musicians will nowadays show much curiosity about Cherubini, whom Beethoven considered by far the greatest composer of his day since the death of Haydn and Mozart. Brahms is recorded to have praised Clementi as a master of free and vital form. Of course Brahms did not mean that this was true of a large number of Clementi's works, but it is quite worth while to search Clementi for evidence of Brahms's grounds for admiration; only I fear that most of us would be too snobbish to arrive independently at Brahms's conclusion. A year or two ago I put Clementi's beautiful little Sonata in F sharp minor into one of my pianoforte recitals, but I took the precaution of representing the composer's name by a question-mark, and divulged it only after the sonata had earned its applause in its own right; but it may safely be guessed that, if the artistic equivalent of a good Clementi or Cherubini were to be stolen from one of our national galleries or sold to America, the resulting outcry would be a front-page topic in our newspapers for months.

I am not pleading that we should devote more attention to our lesser musical masters. On the contrary, it is highly undesirable that in our short lives we should rate time as cheaply as wall-space; and most of the present argument is, in fact, devoted to a warning against the historian's tendency to lose all sense of proportion and to confuse the interest of processes with the permanent values of results. It would be easy, in fact, to turn the whole of the present argument into a diatribe against the notion of progress in art. There is no doubt that it is only in immature states of art that the term 'progress' has the same meaning as it has in science. Elsewhere the use of the term may as well be taken as a symptom of bad criticism. In practice the integrity of music has probably suffered as much from misapplying the notion of progress as from any other artistic fallacy, and certainly such a notion has never been a genuine source of inspiration.

LECTURE V

THERE is no cheaper substitute for criticism than to call whatever we like 'inspired', and to deny inspiration to anything we do not wish to honour with our attention. We are justified in viewing with the gravest suspicion almost every use of the term as an aesthetic criterion. The suspicion should not amount to downright scepticism. Inspiration is one of the most important things in art. And we are told that one of the most fundamental criteria of Persian poetry consists in a clear separation of the spontaneous essential of poetry from the mechanical and intellectual vehicle that may or may not convey it.

In all countries, but more especially in the East, this line of criticism tends to reject all elements in art that can be paraphrased or described in terms of intellectual content and organized form. In our more self-conscious modern Western art, this tendency is beginning to recoil upon itself, for our pursuit of meaningless word-patterns and unrepresentative lines and colours, no less than our repudiations and contradictions of classical methods in music, is becoming more mechanical and self-conscious than any formalism or scholarship. The sources of inspiration lie deep within the subconscious mind, and recent developments of psychology have stimulated many artists to founding their art consciously upon the subconsciousness. Far be it from me to trespass upon the grounds of a science in which I am no expert. That is an enterprise which had better be left to artists; but there is surely no difficulty in seeing a certain inconsistency in expecting that subconsciousness will remain a source of inspiration when it has been exposed. In fact, everybody knows that the essential value of psycho-analysis consists in the fact that, as soon as the subconscious causes of a psychosis have been exposed, the whole trouble vanishes for ever.

It is unreasonable to be disturbed by the discovery that, when a drainage system is exposed, its contents are such as we normally prefer to keep out of sight. Nor, on the other hand, is it comforting to be told that a bad smell cannot be due to the drains, for there are none. But the subconscious mind is the source of the best things as well as of the worst; nor need it be any the worse for inevitably containing everything that is most shocking to our consciousness. Sanitation is one of the noblest applications of science, and its chief beauty is that its work is unseen. There may be difficulty in distinguishing the decent concealments of good sanitation from the deceitful repressions of bad, but no excuse is accepted for failure to make the distinction.

Let me admit once for all that the sources of inspiration are subconscious, but let me at once disclaim any intention of delving into them. My intention is merely to investigate the conditions in which inspiration is possible, and chiefly to remove the prejudices and scruples that arise from accepting too readily a separation between inspired work and *Verstandesarbeit*, or intellectual construction. The condition of an inspired artist working at full speed has often been noted in literature and biography, from

Shakespeare's 'poet's eye in a fine frenzy rolling', to Wagner's account of the terrific impetus which carried him through the score of *Tristan*. Recent fiction has more than once exploited this theme with the profoundly useful and interesting distinction that the inspired heroes and heroines have been described as the authors of unmitigated rubbish. E. F. Benson's *Secret Lives* and Arnold Bennett's *A Great Man*, a work which he ironically acknowledged to be autobiographical, might have been even more corrective and stimulating to artists and critics if they had appeared in time to repair or avert the damage which honest Anthony Trollope did to his own reputation by describing in his autobiography his business-like working habits. When Trollope's autobiography appeared, the artistic temperament was being discovered and its fine frenzy was a mark of respectability which could hardly be too openly displayed. Sciolists, medical and literary, had not yet taken the further step by which artists were more crassly identified with lunatics, a confusion natural enough in persons with a subnormal capacity for art, though such persons cannot be acquitted of a no less gross lack of science in their failure to see the equally profound resemblance between the philistine and the idiot.

Mr. Desmond MacCarthy has pointed out that Trollope in his autobiography confesses to nothing less than a state of inspiration in the way in which his characters occupied his mind with all the force of living experience. The first readers of his autobiography had very little excuse for their snobbery in ignoring this aspect of his work and pouncing upon the evidence that he wrote his novels much as if they were business letters. Much the same might be said of Bach, Handel, and Mozart; and these three cases are remarkable in three different ways. Bach's work is always highly organized, and nearly always evidently rich in its intellectual content: in the immense bulk of Bach's works there are few pages that can be dismissed as unimportant. Mozart's work is always highly finished, though a considerable bulk is perfunctory and unimportant. Handel's work seldom shows any apparatus at all: no great composer has written a larger proportion of rubbish, and no artist has given us so little technical means of distinguishing his rubbish from his greatest achievements.

With these three artists it is evidently quite hopeless to attempt to distinguish what is inspired from what is not inspired. Our impulse is to say that the dull work is uninspired, and that what we like is inspired. By all means let us obey this impulse, but we must not call it criticism. If there were any inherent opposition between conscious intellectual work and spontaneous inspiration we should expect to find that the bulk of Bach's work was uninspired and the bulk of Handel's inspired, but the fact remains that modern criticism finds the bulk of Bach's work inspired in itself and a source of inspiration in others, while even the great heart of the naïve British public idolizes its Handel for the sake of one-fiftieth of that master's output and is accustomed to enjoy even that with the addition of heavy sauces and seasonings.

I will skip a long process of argument, for which you have my word that I have carefully worked it out, and give you at once my own conclusion, which is that Bach, Handel, and Mozart each achieved his enormous output in a continued state of inspiration, and that the inspiration has little or nothing to do with the varying values of the output. A work of art that is merely *Verstandesarbeit*, or intellectual construction, is worthless because it is uninspired; but its lack of inspiration has nothing to do with its being a *Verstandesarbeit*. And, mysterious though the nature of inspiration may be, an inspired work is neither a *Verstandesarbeit* nor a collection of Handelian clichés with the addition of a mysterious divine spark. I find myself driven to the unpalatable and prosaic doctrine that inspiration is indistinguishable from first-rate athletic form, whether mental or physical. The highest achievements of art, of athletics, and of mechanical skill cannot be attained without practice, but are far too complex and subtle to be attained only by practice and reasoned effort. The author of an uninspired *Verstandesarbeit* is as the centipede perspiring in a ditch considering how to crawl. The centipede's inspiration, we are told, had been paralysed by a malicious snail who asked him which leg he put down first; and there is no more effective way of paralysing a skill that already exists than by calling attention to its mechanism. Nothing is easy unless most of it is habitual, and you cannot pick a habit to pieces and begin at any chance point in the middle of its action. There is much to be said for the doctrine that heredity itself is a form of habit, and there is no doubt that the more deep-set a habit is the less capable are we of analysing it, or even of noticing it.

Work that is founded on an insufficient basis of

habit can never seem spontaneous or natural. The uninspired *Verstandesarbeit* fails because all its intellectual processes are insufficient to give it the fluency of habits that have penetrated deep into the subconsciousness. The great heart of the naïve public is as susceptible as the most discerning critic to the signs of work that has attained this ease. Nothing ever became a best-seller without this quality. The best-seller may be contemptible as a work of art, but the brutal truth remains that the most valuable intellectual work will not live unless it has this quality in common with the worst of best-sellers. A work of art that will stand the tests of wholeness and consistency is an achievement far beyond conscious intellectual processes. Its achievement depends upon a mental athletic form that can be attained and preserved only by constant practice on the basis of habits which have long become unconscious. This basis ought to be too firm to be shaken by any effort of the artist to add pioneer work to his mass of ascertained habit. The difference between Bach and Handel consists largely in the fact that Bach is so continually adding pioneer work to his routine that the pioneer work itself rapidly forms into habits, whereas Handel exerts himself only where the Bible and other special circumstances rouse him. Arnold Bennett makes a shrewd critic say of the work of his Great Man that 'This author will never improve'; and the publisher of a prolific writer of best-sellers is haunted by the nightmare lest some educative accident may awaken his lucrative author's powers of self-criticism and reduce him to the condition of the perspiring, self-conscious centipede.

77

Obviously, the inspiration which carried Wagner through the labours of *Tristan* was a force that had grown through a long and severe process of self-criticism. Few artists have, in fact, shown so enormous a development in taste and subtlety of style as Wagner. Wagner's early musical style had a facility which might well have satisfied a less ambitious artist; and might, indeed, have even left him unconscious that anything higher could be achieved. The vulgar popular author often does not know that literature and art contain higher thoughts than his own, and, unless he is a cynical moneymaker, the discovery of this truth would probably dry up his inspiration at the source.

The most miraculous feature in Wagner's development—a feature which is quite unparalleled elsewhere in music—is that his inspiration did prevail over the inhibiting force of a self-criticism that advanced in a few years from the dangerous facility of *Lohengrin* to the uniquely rich new musical language of *Tristan*. The value of a work of art depends as much upon the self-criticism and the conscious work of the artist as upon inspiration. Men of science, such as Helmholtz and Poincaré, have given us vivid accounts of the force of inspiration that accompanied their best work. All such accounts, including the stories of work achieved in dreams, and of problems found solved after a dreamless sleep, agree in two particulars: first, that the decisive steps have eluded the conscious memory; and secondly, that the inspiration has never occurred except as the reward of strenuous work. Poincaré describes the process by the analogy of the molecules of a gas dash-

ing about in a vessel, and he supposes that the disconnected particles of his thoughts, which are far
too numerous and heterogeneous to be deliberately
joined together one by one, will have their chance of
finding their true alliances only when they have been
stirred up into constant agitation. Helmholtz also
finds that *der Einfall*, 'the thing that occurs'—or,
as the excellent slang word expresses it, 'the brain-
wave'—never came to him if there was the slightest
trace of alcohol in his system. There is nothing in-
consistent with this and the fact that many persons
have done their best work under alcoholic stimulus.
There was a time when such persons might have
learned to work much better without alcohol, and
scientific experiments with work which needs attention to complex details but with no scope for original
invention have shown conclusively that pipe-setters,
for example, imagine that they are working better
with the help of alcohol when statistics clearly show
that their speed and accuracy have been reduced by
it. If this is not so with inventive work, that is
because the proverb *in vino veritas* is true, inasmuch
as wine removes inhibitions. A sober man is afraid
of making a fool of himself, and a sober artist whose
self-criticism checks his inspiration will at all events
start his work, if not continue it, more easily if this
check is removed. But there is no reason to resort to
drugs to remove the check. Beethoven has left us the
record of innumerable sketches of almost all his works,
from the smallest to the greatest. Nottebohm, who
published selections from many of Beethoven's sketch-
books, had the wisdom to make a comment that
has been neglected by other pious hero-worshippers

from Sir George Grove onwards. He notices that these sketches show every conceivable variety of method: so much so that we ought to allow for the possibility or probability that in some of the cases where no sketches are to be found Beethoven went to work without making any; but Grove expresses an innocent surprise that the sketches of some of Beethoven's greatest things are often abjectly commonplace, and he fails to connect this with facts equally noteworthy to him, that the handwriting is a vile and rapid scrawl and that the sketches are exceedingly numerous; from which he infers that this admirably illustrates the infinite capacity of genius for taking pains.

Now the crux in that much-abused dictum lies in the contradiction between the idea of taking pains and the idea of an infinite capacity. If you take pains you are straining yourself, but if you have an infinite capacity nothing can be a strain to you. What Beethoven's sketches show is that he did not take pains at the wrong time. He scrawled any cliché that would mark the place where an idea ought to be, and when he had advanced to sketching whole sections of a work, as in the seven or more sketches of half the first movement of the 'Eroica' Symphony, he often found it easier to begin again from the beginning and copy out the unaltered parts of his sketch, so that the act of writing had the same continuity as the flow of his thoughts, rather than tinker at isolated passages. He wrote down what occurred to him as fast as it occurred to him. When he read it over some of it bored him, and he rewrote it easily and quickly with alterations that interested him. He is recorded to have said that this method of scribbling was a bad habit, and doubtless he may sometimes have felt that it was a drag on him. But in all its forms it is a method of a man who thoroughly knows his own mind, and who needs no alcohol to encourage him to put down a crude sketch of his thoughts before he is ready to present them accurately. Contrast this with the method of a friend of mine who long ago in our undergraduate days showed me what he called the sketch of a symphony, in which the only thing that was sketchy was that it was in full score. His process was about as practical as an attempt to construct the Forth Bridge from one rivet to the next.

Beethoven's sketches, whether for a full orchestra or for the lightest pianoforte music, were written at a pace comparable to that of the music; certainly far more rapidly than the pace at which I can dictate these lectures. My friend's symphonic sketch must have taken several hours for a few bars, and the hideous labour of achieving it in the rough could not leave the composer very ready to face the problems of reshaping it. Beethoven could cheerfully make the most radical blunders in his first sketches with the certainty that next day five minutes' work would substitute, if not the right thing, something obviously altered in the right way.

I have sometimes tried to give a lecture on the sketches for the 'Eroica' Symphony, but have found that it could not be dealt with in less than a course of six, or better still ten, lectures. Perhaps I may attempt this some day. At present I will cite the fact that Beethoven's chief difficulty in constructing the opening of this symphony was due to the persistent intrusion of a passage on the dominant for which there was no room in the exposition. Let us consider the exposition in its final form. You see that the momentary cloud which comes over the theme after it has stated its first figure is produced by a chromatic step downwards. In the counterstatement the theme replaces this by a step upwards, which is carried in further sequences till it reaches the dominant. A few bars on the dominant lead to a third statement for full orchestra, in which the theme now moves in two steps of a third which carry it on to the enhanced dominant, by means of which the home tonic is sunk beyond the horizon and the first action of the drama —that is to say, the first radical change of key—is established.

Now Beethoven wrote several sketches of this opening before he could get rid of a tiresome tendency of the main theme to appear on the dominant before its proper third statement. This idea is quite unworkable in the exposition, but the probable reason why it was so importunate in Beethoven's consciousness is that it becomes vitally necessary long afterwards in the recapitulation. The dramatic suspense which precedes the recapitulation is one of the most famous passages in all music, and the cloudy chord in the first statement of the theme is no longer a passing cloud, but the occasion for a most paradoxical modulation. This modulation has its consequences, not less inevitable than itself; and the one thing predestined by Nature to restore the balance is the passage on the dominant which was so intrusive in the first opening.

There is no *Verstandesarbeit* here, or anywhere in the sketches. Inspiration doubtless comes unsought, but it comes only to the artist who has the patience to wait for it, and while waiting to work for it. Doubtless the work is often best directed to side issues. In other words, the watched pot never boils. The astronomer and the microscopist when they wish to see very fine detail form the habit of gazing at a point somewhere to the side of what they wish to see, but their best vision will appear to an unfatigued eye.

There is no justification for saying *a priori* that the technical elaboration of this or that work renders inspiration impossible, any more than there is for saying that a work has not enough organization to be inspired. That which transcends knowledge will never come without knowledge. If the burden of knowledge is too great for the artist, his remedy is not to have less knowledge, but to have more habit and experience in the handling of it. Hence, we constantly find in the genesis of all art, bad and good, that the successful artist is always inspired in the low sense of working easily on the impetus of long habit, and that the deeper and more vivid inspiration will often first appear in matters comparatively accessory. For instance, Shakespeare's early work begins with the use of stock material which did not demand the exercise of his own powers; and to the end of his career he was so easily satisfied with such stock-in-trade devices that, as Dr. Johnson says, to censure his plots is to spend our criticism upon 'unresisting imbecility'. The power of Shakespeare's inspiration first shows itself in minor characters, such as the Nurse in *Romeo and Juliet*, and around such characters the immense and real world of Shakespeare's creation builds itself.

An artist's world must build itself of materials that he knows. A work of art is more vital than a crystal, but many conditions and apparatuses of art are to its vital organization much as a piece of string, a twig, or a twisted wire is to the crystals which will close around it and form a glorious symmetrical object when it is dipped into a saturated solution. Biology and organic chemistry have not achieved, and may perhaps never achieve, the step from crystallization to vital structures, and perhaps it is beyond any power of analysis to distinguish between what is vital in a work of art and what is merely crystalline. But it is not enough to point out that your crystalline object will retain its shape and its beauty when the string or wire round which it built itself has been dissolved or removed.

One of the most beautiful crystalline objects in all music is a certain Psalm by Sweelinck, in which the figures of the tune we know as the Old Hundredth are detached according to the grammatical sense of the words to which the tune is set, and built into a glorious little chorus. In my Deneke lecture on 'Musical Form and Matter' I cited this Psalm as an instance of the way in which matter can be quite inseparable from form. Unfortunately, I am in no position to prove that matter and form are inseparable from inspiration, for this precise crystalline structure or mechanism is used, not only by Sweelinck throughout four volumes of Psalms, but pervades the complete works of Michael Praetorius, a composer whose thirty-fourth volume has just reached me, and in whose pages I regret to say that I have not yet been able to find any inspiration whatever. Perhaps other students may have found greater patience rewarded by greater luck, and may be able to quote Praetorius as an inspired artist. I am quite certain that great inspiration is invariably accompanied by great skill. The technique of Handel's dullest work is not as great as that of his finest. In neither case does it consist in devices that are recognized as subjects of academic study, and in Bach's works the technique lies mainly in such subjects; but in the work which we can distinguish as inspired the technique differs from that of dull work in an uncanny accuracy and thoroughness.

The D sharp minor and A minor Fugues of *Das Wohltemperirte Klavier* which I quoted in an earlier lecture are, with all respect to Bach and to the text-books which cite them with reverence, manifestly imperfect in technique, and they more than exhaust the possibilities of their subjects, because their ugli-nesses ought not to have existed; and I have already shown that the great B flat minor Fugue is the closest of at least eight other fugues that could have been made on the same scheme, and the work of Bach which is still supposed to be merely a technical exercise, *Die Kunst der Fuge*, is uninspired only where its technical problems are inherently those of a mere exercise. Wherever the problems are normal to the material the result is as noble as anything Bach ever wrote; and though we have every reason to think that the scheme of *Die Kunst der Fuge* is nearly com-plete, its actual technical possibilities are incalculably more numerous than the selections which Bach can possibly have intended to work out.

Every serious analysis of works of art reveals an uncanny accuracy and thoroughness when the work is what is called inspired. When the technical apparatus is not that by which students can be trained our analysis must not look for academic devices. Handel is undoubtedly a supreme master of counterpoint, and Shakespeare a supreme master of dramatic construction; but to analyse Handel's fugues as if they were Bach's and Shakespeare's plays as if they were French *pièces bien faites* is, to quote Johnson again, to expend criticism on unresisting imbecility. The only discoverable thread that is available for the analysis of a masterpiece of Handel is much the same as that by which you may hope to unravel the mysteries of Bach's Chromatic Fantasia, or the Organ Fantasia in G minor. These are in the main supremely accurate examples of a musical rhetoric. Stanford's favourite illustration from Handel is the aria 'Total eclipse' in *Samson*, of which Stanford has given a beautiful analysis in his little primer of composition.

It might be possible to misunderstand the conventions which are the working hypotheses of such music. Milton, of whose *Samson Agonistes* the libretto of Handel's oratorio is a ghastly travesty, would have had great difficulty in foreseeing the conventions of an art two generations later than his own; and Tennyson, who objected to song-writers who made him say twice what he had said only once, would probably have made the same objection to the symmetrical scheme which compels Handel to repeat the words; but the more intimately we know such a masterpiece

86

the more necessary and less obtrusive its conventions appear. The repetitions present us with newer and deeper aspects of the words, and the complete impression of the whole excludes as irrelevant all the distress that we must feel at the librettist's travesty of Milton, and vindicates the authentic voice of Milton in a music as great as *Samson Agonistes* itself.

LECTURE VI

ONE of our chief concerns to-day is to vindicate the integrity of music in opera. The student of opera can learn much from Dean Church's paradox that it is unscientific to apply the terms 'higher' and 'lower' to the criticism of poetry. The terms have a meaning which is as true within its limits as the terms 'pure' and 'mixed'. Opera is an art in which music cannot possibly be unmixed. But there is no reason why music-drama should not have its integrity. As Moth puts it in *Love's Labour Lost*, 'I am sure you know how much the gross sum of deuce-ace amounts to'. *Armado*: 'It doth amount to one more than two.' *Moth*: 'Which the base vulgar do call three.'

Let us not rest contented with the euphuistic Don Adriano de Armado's habit of leaving his elements unintegrated, and let us have no snobbish reluctance to use the language of the 'base vulgar' when it is more adequate than that of the superior person. The terms 'higher' and 'lower' are conveniently, though dangerously, applicable to conditions in which an art is free to develop in full concentration or restricted by a mixture of elements. If there is any sense in saying that a string quartet is a higher form of art than a symphony, this can only mean that a string quartet can achieve by the economic use of its four instruments music as important as that which a symphony achieves by a great number of instruments that lose their individuality in the orchestral crowd.

From this we may infer a presumption that the composer who can find his freedom in the string quartet is more capable of producing pure music—or, as I prefer to put it, that his pure music will have more integrity—than the composer who cannot satisfy himself with less than an orchestra.

We may also expect that in a census of string quartets and symphonies there will be a smaller proportion of low-grade string quartets than of low-grade symphonies—that, in fact, the prolific writer of string quartets will be a more high-minded composer than the prolific writer of symphonies; but all such statistics are troublesome work, the results of which may be unscrupulously used. The simple fact is that the composer of a string quartet has less temptations to be vulgar than the composer who deals with a more luxurious apparatus; but the dangers of a facile classification of art into 'higher' and 'lower' begin to outweigh the advantages when an art-form has obvious temptations for vulgar artists. The majority of concertos are vulgar, and there is a middle class of concertos, headed by Mendelssohn's masterpiece for the violin, which represent a very pleasant light form of art. But it is nothing less than disgraceful that critics should ever have allowed the technical needs and possibilities of the concerto to induce them to impute the resulting average vulgarities to the supreme masterpieces of concerto style.

The variation form is another case of an art-form which is contemptibly easy to handle for purposes of vulgar display, and the result is that we constantly meet persons of some musical culture who tell us that they do not like variations. This may be in some cases a matter of taste which there is no disputing, but it is far more likely to be an ignorant prejudice; and, indeed, the quasi-technical utterances of many critics and musical commentators have often displayed a radical misunderstanding of the nature of the variation form. The forms of concertos and variations are prominent among the few cases where it is advisable to have an idea of a generalized notion of a form as a thing true or false in itself. As a rule, no kind of criticism does more injustice to the integrity of art than that which objects to a work as not being a true example of the form it professes. If the work justifies its existence on its own terms its title may be regarded as an external matter; and if a large number of inherently satisfactory works are called by the name of an art-form from which they agree to differ, in the same way we must recognize their agreement by admitting that the name includes this different type. Thus, the meaning of the word 'sonata' is very different for Haydn, Mozart, and Beethoven from what it is for Bach; and both meanings are equally definite, far more definite than the original meaning of the term, which was simply the opposite of 'cantata', a piece that was sounded as distinct from a piece that was sung. But it seems legitimate, and even convenient, to talk of 'true' and 'false' forms when the name of an art-form is primarily associated with masterpieces constructed on definite lines, but has become applied to occasions for all manner of flimsiness and vulgarity. Those modern concertos which are not vulgar are for the most part in a much lighter form than that of the concertos of Mozart, Beethoven, and Brahms; but the true concertos of those three composers constitute such a mere handful in comparison with what exists for good and for evil elsewhere that it might seem rather precious to restrict the notion of a true concerto to so small a handful; yet the preciousness might be justified by the fact that these few concertos are among the sublimest achievements of pure music, whereas even the best of the lighter forms of concerto are manifestly nothing of the kind.

The case of the variation form is equally difficult, and here one of the commonest errors of criticism consists in the despising of the simpler kinds of variation. When we are told that good musicians deplore the frivolity of the choral variations in Beethoven's Ninth Symphony, we had better disregard the critic's claim to know what a good musician is. Those variations are open to criticism, but not to the charge of frivolity. The fact that variations consisting of simple embroidery of the melody can be achieved cheaply and nastily is no reason why Beethoven in the *Sonata Appassionata*, the Violin Concerto, and several other works should not achieve some of his ultimate sublimities in the terms of embroidery variation that provoke the derision of the late Monsieur Vincent d'Indy. On the other hand, variations may be based on other elements than the external melody; and so the strictest and most highly organized of variations on a deeper structural basis may be so unlike the original melody as to mislead not only critics, but composers, into the idea that where the melody is not apparent anything will do.

Two false criteria have thus arisen: one, that it

91

is a defect in a set of variations if the listener cannot trace the melody; the other, that where the melody cannot be traced anything may happen. It is often said that great progress has been made in the varia-. tion form since Beethoven. I have not time here to deal further with this dictum than to say roundly that it is not true. I do not know why the true variation form should be obsolete; nor is there, in fact, any reason why the neglect of an art-form by one generation of composers should prevent its rediscovery by later composers. The composer of variations is nowadays generally at a loose end, and most modern variations have little power to convince us of their reason for existing. A clear, or even a crude, notion of a real difference between true and false variations might be a great stimulus to modern composers.

Both the composition and criticism of opera are at the present day in a condition of better health and better information than the composition and criticism of pure music. When we have succeeded in excluding from our view of opera the dangerous idea that it represents a lower form of art than pure music, we still need to insist upon certain truths which have given rise to the use of that dangerous term. There is a widespread tendency, both popular and academic, to assume that the musical style of opera is more emotional than that of instrumental music. Thus, for instance, Sir Henry Hadow in the *Oxford History of Music* tells us that *Fidelio* is dramatic only as the D minor Sonata is dramatic, implying unmistakably that he thinks that instrumental music is less dramatic than opera. This is far from being the case. 'Staginess' cannot properly be a term of reproach for the stage itself. But we shall find that what is the matter with staginess off the stage is not that it seems exaggerated, but that it seems cold and flimsy. The intensity and concentration of an easel picture would be invisible on the stage, and would hardly become intelligible if the picture were magnified to the dimensions of the stage; but, conversely, stage scenery seen by daylight in a picture gallery consists of colours splashed on flat boards out of a pail, and it is only a freak of fashion that nowadays allows something almost as crude as stage make-up to conceal real human complexions in daylight.

All the intensity of Wagner's ripest style does not reach the heat of a climax in a work comparatively so statuesque as Brahms's F minor Pianoforte Quintet. I shall never forget my surprise when, being haunted by a passage in that work, I found myself trying to place it somewhere in Wagner or Verdi before I discovered where it really belonged. Mozart, the only composer who divided his time almost equally between opera and absolute music and achieved perfect integrity in both, gives us a clear illustration of the relative values of stage emotion and symphonic emotion in the fight between Don Giovanni and the Commendatore, which is perfectly represented with complete adequacy. But in one of his mature symphonies such a music would sound drily formal, and an instrumental style that does not constantly rise beyond it inadequately represents Mozart's symphonic style at the age of fifteen. This, then, is the sense in which opera may be considered a lower form of art. But we must not call that art 'low' which perfectly integrates the enormous mass of material that constitutes an opera.

With Mozart the integration is so perfect that it has had paradoxical results in the ups and downs of performance and criticism of his operas. The first thing that became obvious to the meanest capacity was that, though Mozart was doubtless a great composer, his librettists were contemptible as poets and dramatists. Hence, not only the criticism and performance, but the editors of Mozart's operas, even in what is still the standard critical edition, scorned to qualify themselves for dealing with opera at all. The standard full-scores of *Die Entführung*, of *Die Zauberflöte*, and of Beethoven's *Fidelio* appear in the so-called critical edition without any of the spoken dialogue. It is true that as literature the spoken dialogue is beneath criticism, and it is equally true that in its purely musical aspects the music is already beyond praise; but the editors and the practical improvers of the words and action ought to have known that the music which was so far beyond their praise was even farther beyond their understanding if they did not condescend to take it in its integrity— that is to say, its integrity with the words. And it was the professional musicians who were at fault in this matter. The great Mozart-lover Otto Jahn acquired his immense knowledge of music in the course of a lifetime devoted to classical scholarship. Jahn's *Persius* is a monument of Latin scholarship, even more famous among classical scholars than his Mozart biography is among musicians. He, then, of all persons might have been expected to despise and neglect Mozart's libretti; but, being a first-rate scholar, he committed no such blunder, and his accounts of Mozart's operas, including all that Mozart wrote from the age of twelve upwards, invariably begin with a thorough précis and criticism of the action.

We need not set against this the notorious fact that Jahn was a vitriolic anti-Wagnerian. A man whose affections are as strong and whose knowledge of what he loves is as profound as Jahn's may be forgiven if he has violent prejudices against what impresses not only him, but the world at large, as opposed to what he loves. But charity does not require us to forgive the iniquities committed by a tepid orthodoxy that in the editing of a great classic avowedly acts in contemptuous neglect, and even deliberate suppression, of aspects which were matters of deep concern to the composer.

The intelligent study of Mozart owes much of its impetus on the Continent to Richard Strauss, and in England to Professor Dent, who some years before the late War had a great share in an epoch-making performance of *Die Zauberflöte* at Cambridge, and whose book on Mozart's operas is one of the most important landmarks in English musical literature. The technical difficulties of Mozart's operatic roles are so great that we need not wonder that for a while progress in the renascence of Mozart was more evident in the better understanding of the libretti than in the musical standards of performance. One witty critic went so far as to write an article on da Ponte at the Old Vic in which he jibed at the imminent danger lest the librettist should be regarded as greater than the composer. That danger is past. Nothing will make da Ponte and

Schikaneder accepted as great poets; and, whatever primitive conditions we may tolerate in scenery and costumes, or even in the acting, of Mozart's operas, all regard it as self-evident that the singing must be as perfect as lies in human power. It has become as fashionable to go to Salzburg and Glyndebourne for our Mozart as to go to Bayreuth for Wagner, and at Glyndebourne and Salzburg it is taken for granted that the action of Mozart's operas must be worked out as carefully as if Mozart, like Wagner, were his own librettist. Da Ponte and Schikaneder were past-masters of stagecraft; and we may doubt whether Mozart could have been as successful with dramas of greater intrinsic value unless he had been his own librettist. There is some parallel between his case and those of Irving and Sarah Bernhardt, who in several instances won their greatest triumphs in plays, like *The Bells* and *Fédora*, that fitted them but fitted no one else, and had, indeed, but flimsy reasons for existing.

Mozart was fortunate, not only in the ready-to-hand stagecraft of his librettists, but also in the fact that they were bulliable and that he knew how to bully them. In this respect Beethoven's bad luck was almost tragic. *Fidelio* is a very much greater opera than orthodoxy is as yet ready to admit, and its defects, both in its almost impossible earlier form as the *Leonore* of 1806 and in its final form as the *Fidelio* of 1814, are not, as is still commonly thought, the result of Beethoven's habits as a purely instrumental composer, but are the defects of the important school of French opera that culminated in Cherubini, whom Beethoven regarded as the greatest composer of his time.

As a magnificent tale of heroism the plot of *Fidelio* would impress everyone as it impressed Beethoven, if only it had been reasonably clearly told. It is the chief example of several similar products of the French Revolution, being the story of a heroic wife who rescues her husband from the fate of a political prisoner. Many lectures would be needed to show how Beethoven's difficulties arose and how they spring from no fault in his music, but are the direct results of a conflict between French operatic forms and a subject which has developed a power beyond their scope; but the important conclusion reached by all study of the vicissitudes through which *Fidelio* attained its final form is that Beethoven learned by experience, what he would have learned from Mozart if Mozart's subjects had been ostensibly more serious, that music for the stage must live at a much lower temperature than purely instrumental music. The mighty overtures designed for *Leonore* in its first and second productions were inadmissible in *Fidelio*, and the modern custom of inserting *Leonore No. 3* as a prelude to the second act is a dangerous concession to musical self-indulgence.

I have used the metaphor of temperature for this question of musical values. But there are other intensities than that of temperature, and we need set no limits to the depth that is attainable in music for the theatre. While the temperature of *Fidelio* is consistently reduced at every point from that of *Leonore*, the depth is as consistently increased; and the listener need not trouble to explain the paradox that the emotional effect of *Fidelio* is point for point incomparably greater than that of *Leonore*.

Jahn is of opinion that Beethoven in 1814 was out of sympathy with the *Leonore* of 1806, that his revision of it does not do justice to the earlier ideas, and that it introduces marked discrepancies into the style. Here the philologist is too wise after the event. Nobody appreciating *Fidelio* in the light of pure instrumental enjoyment or integral musical dramatic enjoyment would ever regard as a discrepancy the fact that the most pathetic moments in this music-drama coincide with the deepest music. Still less would he impute the extra depth to a discrepancy of date, or feel the slightest concern how and why these most pathetic passages were the most beautiful. The only matter that is of interest here is a matter beyond the scope of *Fidelio*. I believe it is a measurable fact that from 1814 onwards Beethoven's purely instrumental style develops, besides its ever increasing polyphony, a certain tendency to let its moments of action occur explosively after long periods of exposition. All drama shows this tendency as it develops. However severely the dramatist may economize every word for the purposes of action, it is mainly by words that drama explains itself. Pageantry and mime without words are not more, but less, dramatic and emotionally less exciting than the drama which, relying increasingly upon dialogue, presents to us the elements of a crisis slowly and surely ripening towards the point where a sudden action explodes the whole situation.

Purely instrumental music had, as I have already pointed out, long lived consistently at a far higher temperature than theatre music; but this question of the slow incubation and explosive determination of dramatic action is not a question of temperature. After *Fidelio*, Beethoven's purely instrumental music certainly did not become more theatrical, but it did become deeper in ways which I believe he learned when he found out how to deepen the pathos of Florestan's music in the dungeon scene. It is not of the slightest importance whether my impression is a case of *post hoc ergo propter hoc*. Beethoven may have been able to increase the pathos of Florestan because his instrumental style was deepening, or the two tendencies may have merely coincided, as far as they did coincide, in time. Of course, we can cite as circumstantial evidence that the revision of *Fidelio* coincides with the production of two theatrical *pièces d'occasion*, *King Stephen* and *The Ruins of Athens*; and it is certain that an eminent critic devoted a weighty article to accusing Beethoven of a disquieting tendency to rely more and more on stage effects. The obvious correct answer to this is that staginess should not be used as a term of abuse for what belongs to the stage. Beethoven was naughty enough, as I have seen with my own eyes, to scrawl on the pages of this criticism an entirely unprintable statement as to the relative value of the critic's highest thoughts and biological waste-products, which Beethoven implicitly identifies with these insolent and perfunctory *pièces d'occasion*.

In these matters most of us know too much about drama and fiction. Drama and fiction are actually too true to life, and a man under genuine stress of emotion may possibly, though let us hope not often, be inhibited from saying what is perfectly natural to him because it is what would be said by a character in the same situation in a novel or play. In the same way, a lover of music may be less apt to misjudge the values of instrumental music if he is not experienced in opera; and as instrumental music is, speaking loosely and dangerously, much the higher and purer form of art, or, speaking accurately, much the severer in its demands on the intelligence, we shall probably find a better musical taste prevalent among lovers of instrumental music who dislike opera than among persons devoted to opera. For this very reason it is necessary to be specially on our guard against the prejudices of instrumental purists. If, when listening to a string quartet, we are so foolish as to regret that it gives us none of the thrills of opera, we shall be incapable of receiving from it the thrills that it can give to an intelligent listener. On higher grounds, we come to the fact that the string quartet is a much more ethereal and subtle medium than the symphony; and from this we can easily see that the typical vice of a bad string quartet is that it imitates an orchestra. But here, again, our knowledge may be misapplied, and we may blame a string quartet for succeeding in sounding like an orchestra. If it achieves that, it cannot have been orchestrally written at all. String-quartet writing that succeeds in sounding orchestral is magnificent, but if it were transcribed literally for the orchestra it would not sound orchestral, and I have no very clear idea of anything in earth or heaven that it would resemble. Bad orchestral writing for a string-quartet is writing that assumes that four stringed instruments scraping away in the elementary fashion which is often the noblest economy in an orchestra will sound as if the four solo players were engaged in tasks worthy of their eminence.

Similar confusions of thought arise in discussing the relation between the organ and the orchestra. The style of organ-playing and organ-composition is often ruined by an all-pervading tendency to make the organ imitate the instruments of an orchestra, a habit which destroys the noble architectural character of the genuine organ and reveals the mechanical voices of its masqueradings.

We unfortunately know that Bruckner was a great organist; and nothing is easier for the critic to detect than the organ-like habits of his orchestral compositions; but to say that he orchestrates like an organist is to say precisely the thing which is not. He orchestrates like a master of the orchestra; and, inasmuch as he succeeds in making the orchestra sound like an organ, he succeeds in producing from it the noblest sounds that he can imagine.

Jealous champions of purity should beware lest they forget that all instruments and all musical art-forms rest on the common ground of music, and that those forms and instruments which have the widest musical range can only lose their own integrity and the integrity of music by confining themselves each within the range of what no other resource can imitate. Let me repeat an illustration which I have often used: that conversation would be unnaturally restricted if the arbiters of taste were to enforce upon us that no lady should say anything that could possibly be said by a gentleman, and no gentleman say anything that could possibly be said by a lady.

LECTURE VII

THERE is a dangerous clearness in the appearance of musical art-forms to those who can read music like books, and who can follow a technical analysis. We need not be sceptical as to the positive facts that are so easily discoverable by the analysis of individual works; but the statistical results of a large number of works are always misleading. This is partly because in art the average is always false. The only thing that matters in a work of art is the individual work, and every actuary knows that he cannot tell whether a selected individual will fall within his statistical averages, even if that individual seems already doomed by actually suffering from the causes covered by the statistics. The epicure who was assured by the doctor that his over-indulgence in lampreys would kill him promptly defeated the doctor by eating an enormous meal of the forbidden food and then throwing himself from the top of a tower in order to die from some other cause.

The apparent rigidity of musical art-forms is not merely a statistical illusion. When we are duly attending to an individual work we are in danger of drawing unsound inferences from the way in which the printed page represents symmetries that exist in time by symmetries that exist on paper. Much of our appreciation of architecture and painting depends upon the *coup d'œil*, the instantaneous and abiding impression of a thing entirely comprised in one field of vision. In architecture there are also symmetries which are not so comprised, and which demand that we should use our memory in order to appreciate the correspondence of the right side with the left; but even in these cases there is nothing to prevent us from going over the ground again; and, moreover, we are often supposed not only to do this, but to view our architecture at different distances. Our knowledge of an architectural work is an accumulation of many views, and perhaps none of these has any claim to be *the* main view. There is no point of view from which you can see all round a building, but as we approach a building we first come to a point at which a whole façade gives immediate pleasure, and at the same distance there are various views combining two sides at various angles. The architect of the Paris Opera fell into tragic despair when he found that he had miscalculated in this matter, and that his dome was not visible at the only possible first approach to the façade. There is a similar, though less fatal, defect in St. Peter's at Rome.

As we approach nearer to a building the views of whole facades extend beyond our sight, and the architect has to satisfy us with more and more detail. His art consists in contriving that at distant points of view his finer detail will not confuse his great lines, and that at nearer points of view the great lines will not be bald and tiresome. Roughly speaking, the eye will receive an impression of grand proportions in whatever is designed to fill its field, whether the view is distant or near.

There is no exact parallel to this in music. There might be, and the cinematograph might do something to develop it, if we were more in the habit of enjoying a thing which gives me personally much pleasure—the progressive change in the aspect of a building as you walk round it, the appearance of actual movement as perspectives open and close and features are gradually revealed and concealed. The symmetries of music all exist thus in motion, and the direction of that motion is unalterably fixed. There is no exact parallel in music to the mirror relation between the right and left halves of a symmetrical object. Optical symmetry demands that the right and left sides should face each other in opposition, but you cannot treat time thus. Music becomes unintelligible if you turn it backwards; and even the mis-spent ingenuity by which a musical phrase may be designed to bear the process, though it may make the backwards phrase intelligible, will not make it recognizable.

The symmetries of music are at least as powerful and necessary as those of architecture. But we must never lose sight of the fact that their real existence is in our memory, and that our power of verifying them by sight on the written page is a matter external to the music and apt to give both critics and composers misleading information. The most prominent feature in clearly constructed music is that of re-capitulation. In music it is the main means of symmetry, and the musical recapitulations are at least as exact and extensive as those of architecture. They are quite without parallel in words. The symmetries of poems are omnipresent in the details of metre, but extended verbal recapitulation is quite exceptional. The correspondence of strophe and antistrophe in a Greek chorus is minute and highly musical, but is again metrical rather than topical. The parallelism of Hebrew poetry is again a matter of detail. It consists in stating a thing twice in other words. Musical recapitulation is not in other words, and is a matter of extended passages.

Much easy criticism, and some conscientiously free musical composition, has been devoted to the task of emancipating music from the conventions of recapitulation. Martyrs to this cause have been misled by the fatal ease with which musical recapitulation can be traced on paper. Such martyrs have no true idea either of the exactness or of the freedom of good musical recapitulations. In a story or drama recapitulations may be as extensive as in music, but they are not recapitulations of words. They are summaries of former events in words appropriate to a description of the past and not to an announcement of the present.

Exact verbal recapitulation would produce either an exceptional effect or none at all. You will find an exceptional effect of intense musical power towards the end of *Paradise Lost*, where Milton achieves the highest pathos and beauty in describing first how Adam and Eve resolve to go to the place where God had pronounced judgement on them and there express their penitence and pray for pardon; and then, a few paragraphs later, tells us in the same words, with only the necessary change of persons and tenses, that Adam and Eve did so. But it lies in the nature of music to recapitulate long sections note for note. Wagner proves this more conclusively than any other composer, and he proves it in spite of his own indiscreet utterances on the subject. He points out as a defect in Beethoven's Overture *Leonore No. 3* that the trumpet-call which foreshadows the climax of the opera does not fulfil its function in the overture inasmuch as Beethoven is compelled by the rules of sonata form to follow it by a formal recapitulation. It is astonishing that Wagner, who is one of the greatest masters of recapitulation in all musical history, should have allowed himself to make so cheap and unscrupulous a debating-point. He ignores the fact that in *Leonore No. 2* the trumpet-call really was the climax of the overture, in which it immediately precipitated matters and was followed by a coda that did no more than wind matters up with reasonable breadth; but in *Leonore No. 3* the trumpet-call is not the climax, either in fact or in purpose. As compared with *Leonore No. 2*, everything up to the trumpet-call has been drastically compressed to two-thirds of the original length and consistently lowered in temperature. The trumpet-call is the signal for the release of all the pent-up emotions which Beethoven feels in contemplating, not merely the incidents of the drama, but the whole character of Leonora and the glorious ideals of wedded love. The trumpet-call is not immediately followed by the recapitulation. On the contrary, it comes little more than half-way through the development; and the first great climax of the overture is the return to the home tonic, which is a much more exciting affair than any possible effect of an off-stage trumpet. The recapitulation, though spacious, provides by the contemplation of its symmetry no more than a necessary relief during which the mind recovers energy for one of the most enormous codas Beethoven ever wrote. Beethoven has, in fact, set his music free—so free that he had eventually to discard the *Leonore* Overture altogether, because it killed any conceivable stage music. Nothing could be more impertinent than to suggest that Beethoven would let a musical conventionality stand as an obstacle to a dramatic truth. The very critics who are ready to accuse him of this still cling fondly to the delusion that as an instrumental writer he inherited classical art-forms from Haydn and Mozart and broke them by subversive innovations. To believe this may be orthodox, but it shows an encyclopedic ignorance of the classical art-forms, and of what constitutes a classic. To speak of Haydn and Mozart as if they represented a single set of classical conventions is as absurd as to bracket Browning with Tennyson. I do not mean this as a parallel in any less general respect than the absurdity of supposing that the members of each pair resemble each other in habits and methods.

A further question is: Who are the classics? History, as the authors of *1066 and All That* have told us, being what you remember, we are told that the classics of sonata form are Haydn, Mozart, and Beethoven. Their contemporaries did not think so. At all events they thought of them as we think of Strauss, Elgar, and Sibelius. It is more than any living composer's reputation is worth to be accused to-day of anything more orthodox than a strictly private new aesthetic system of his own, but in the time of Beethoven correctness was the chief criterion in all the arts: and a very much better and more stimulating criterion it is than our sterilizing criteria of originality.

Surely it is obvious that the procedures of the greatest masters should not be ruled out of court in favour of averages taken from the works of artists whom we all remember, if at all, only as persons wise in their own generation. I suppose that Spohr and Hummel represent the traditions of sonata form without the disconcerting variety and range of Beethoven's methods; although, if you have the curiosity and patience to study Spohr and Hummel, you will find that both of those masters tried experiments of which the face value amounts to interesting innovations. Spohr's cloying mannerisms are not tiresome enough to destroy the affection which every violinist must feel for so great a master of his instrument; and if, as some eminent critics have been rash enough to say, it is essential to a great composer that he should be a prolific inventor of significant and beautiful themes, Spohr's rank must be high indeed. But Spohr's limitations are so obvious that many musicians whose ear for rhyme has not been cultivated are content merely to regard 'Spohr' as a rhyme for 'bore'. Still, Spohr represents, decidedly better than Mozart and infinitely better than Haydn, the only possible type of a classic if we assume that any of Beethoven's innovations represent a break from classical tradition. Fortunately, Spohr has himself given crushing evidence of the unsoundness of such a view of classical form. Joachim told me that Spohr once said to him: 'I wish some day to write a set of six string quartets all in the regular classical form.' Joachim asked in astonishment in what way Spohr's existing quartets were not regular classical examples. 'No,' said Spohr, 'I mean with shakes at the ends of the passages.'

Spohr's most affectionate friends never accused him of a sense of humour. What is the classical meaning of a shake at the end of a passage? There is nothing contemptible about the device. The sonata style is not the only one in which passages of sustained melody and of polyphonic development need to be relieved by lighter passages tending towards bravura. When your passage of more or less brilliant semiquavers has continued long enough how are you to bring it to an end? Your rapid motion must come to a climax; and you may think fit to interrupt it, or you may prefer a device by which an actual increase of movement closes it automatically. Your brilliant passage may be conventional, but the classical convention, at least in violin music, prefers rapid melody with some kind of transcendental vocal quality to arpeggio figures with no singable element. The pianoforte offers the composer temptations to devices more mechanical and glittering, and it is dreadful to see Mozart's most gifted pupil, Hummel, specializing more and more exclusively in the pianoforte, and carrying us more and more into a world filled with the musical equivalent of glass chandeliers; but, whether your style is that of a glass chandelier or that of a coloratura singer, your passage will come to its most natural conclusion by changing its forward movement to a stationary vibration, more rapid than anything else—in fact, indefinitely rapid. And this we call a trill.

The passage ending with a trill is thus a natural device, which may be expected to become a regular classical feature. The question now arises: in what classics did Spohr find it? Undoubtedly in Mozart, whom Spohr very sensibly regarded as the ideal master. But Spohr was no scholar, and long before his ideas of classical music had become settled Mozart's string quartets were known only in the last ten masterpieces. Thus we may rule out of account all Mozart's earlier works; and we must certainly rule out of account all Haydn's works of any period, for Haydn is one of the most irregular artists that ever wrote.

Now let us see what superlative lies can be told by statistics. In the only string quartets of Mozart that concerned Spohr there are nineteen opportunities for the regular passage ending in a shake. In fourteen —that is to say, in three-quarters of these cases— no such phenomenon occurs. On the other hand, it does occur in the trio of a minuet where there is normally no room for anything of the kind.

Let us return to the subject of recapitulation. Wagner's theories of dramatic declamation were put forward by him with a certain crassness intelligible to the public and suited to the crude controversies which his music provoked. And it seems self-evident that Wagner's treatment of words differs from the classics by its complete realism. You can learn from his music how his words ought to be spoken if there were no music at all. The pace of all singing tends to be slower than that of speaking, and in *Lohengrin* the declamation undoubtedly drags; but in Wagner's mature works from *Das Rheingold* onwards the slowness of the dramatic action is inherent in the huge scale of Wagner's designs, and the handling of speech is as quick as articulate singing permits. Hence, not only the naïve, but the Wagnerian listener may enjoy the works for years without noticing that recapitulations in the music are at least as extensive and exact as in any classical symphony. They happen, not according to the quasi-gravitational forces and symmetries of instrumental music, but according to the opportunities of drama. The singer usually fails to notice them, because the voice parts are with rare exceptions not the vehicles of the main musical substance, but are demonstrably invented by Wagner after the self-completed musical design in the instrumental background. This is sometimes an actual weakness in Wagner's aesthetic system and is at best a legitimate technical expedient which ought never to have been erected into a guiding principle. It does not always represent Wagner's own practice. In most of the first act of *Die Walküre* the voice parts contain the essence of Wagner's musical invention; but in a large proportion of Wagner's work, certainly in more than half, the music is in the orchestra and the voices are talking, in gloriously musical terms, but still with the effect of something written over the surface of a picture. Isolde's *Liebestod* is a magnificent piece of music; but not only singers, but commentators, have been known to analyse it into its single leitmotives without noticing that it is an exact recapitulation of the last movement of the love duet in the second act. Up to the catastrophe, a conductor could conduct the *Liebestod* from the second act with the sole difference that he has to beat four slow beats instead of two quick ones and that he takes rather slower tempi.

The *Liebestod* is a favourite concert piece for orchestra. How does the orchestral arrangement provide for the part of Isolde? It simply leaves her out. Liszt, in his wonderful arrangement of the piece as a pianoforte solo, has included six independent notes of Isolde's near the beginning. Surely the last notes of the singer in this overwhelming swan-song should be memorable. They are the right notes, and they sound supremely beautiful; but I question whether many who know Isolde's *Liebestod* by heart could quote them. As a recapitulation the *Liebestod* is quite as long as the longest in all symphonic movements, that in the first movement of Beethoven's 'Eroica' Symphony. There are plenty of other examples in Wagner's works, not self-evident lyrics like the *Preislied* in *Die Meistersinger*, but pages of solid dramatic development: self-explanatory in the most stupendous case of all, that in *Götterdämmerung* where Siegfried entertains his treacherous enemies with an account of his early life, and, when dying of the murderer's stab, finishes his tale with recapitulating the awakening of Brünnhilde. The fact is that Wagner is one of the supreme masters of purely musical form, but the integrity of his art makes this form arise out of the conditions of his music-drama.

We are apt to be misled as to the nature of musical recapitulation by the practical fact that it necessitates a large amount of mechanical copying. The publisher André once told Mendelssohn in shocked tones that he had seen Beethoven's Seventh Symphony in progress in manuscript, and that Beethoven was evidently composing in a manner that could not but produce disconnected results by leaving many pages blank and skipping from one part of a work to another; to which Mendelssohn replied by playing the Seventh

Symphony until André had to confess himself too delighted to criticize further. André's remarks were quite unworthy of the intelligence of a man who published a score of Mozart's *Zauberflöte* Overture distinguishing in red print the parts which a paler ink in the autograph had shown to be filled in later. It is obvious common sense to put off the mechanical labour of writing a recapitulation when you already know how to attack your coda and are anxious to get to work on it; and it is not only wasting labour, but risking serious inaccuracy, if you do not have your original statement before you when you write its recapitulation. It is extraordinary how the finest details that have occurred to you in the heat of writing will desert your memory if you have mislaid your manuscript. Moreover, the fact that most of your recapitulation can be mechanically copied is no hindrance whatever to your power of making vital changes in the finer details. On the contary, the first condition of the finest subtleties is that the rest shall be accurate. The difference between a true recapitulation and a mechanical one is precisely this, that the composer is aware of the difference between a memory and a first impression. When Siegfried describes from memory how, after tasting the dragon's blood, he understood the language of the birds, he remembers the bird's theme and message, but the orchestra does not remember the high harmonics of the violas and violoncellos.

The dull composer is often content to copy mechanically. He is perhaps more often persuaded by a stupid cleverness to do worse, and to alter for the sake of altering, regardless of the possibility that, if a passage is not necessary the second time, there may be some doubt whether it was necessary the first. The great artist recapitulates with the liveliest consciousness of the difference that memory and other circumstances make. Sometimes it is necessary, as in that case of Siegfried, to show that the memory is a pale reflection of what had originally happened. Sometimes, and perhaps more often, the function of a recapitulation is, as it were, to make us see with two eyes what we had originally seen only with one. This is especially the case where the beauty is that of a sonata-like symmetry. Music, as I have pointed out, cannot be recognized when it is turned backwards; but music finds some analogy to the right and left opposition that we see in symmetrical objects when it recapitulates in the home tonic, or in some symmetrically contrasted key, what had first been heard in a foreign key. In order to produce the material in the home tonic instead of a foreign key, some change is necessary in the transition between the first and second group of material. Now in binocular vision we obtain our impression of solidity through the effort unconsciously made to bring together in a single impression the retinal pictures of each eye. If these pictures were absolutely identical, the resulting impression would be flat; but they are not identical: there is a distinct parallax for nearer objects against the background of more distant ones.

With musical recapitulations, the memory combines its first and second impression in a way not unlike that of the parallax of binocular vision. In any case, a second impression cannot be the same as the first, and the most sensitive composer may find that the mere fact of its being a second impression provides all the difference that is needed; but I doubt whether in any vital piece of work there is such a thing as a completely flat recapitulation. The alterations may be very minute and subtle, but they almost always have in common the demonstrable fact that the second impression is more solid than the first. My favourite *locus classicus* is a single bar from the first movement of Mozart's String Quartet in E flat —the ninth bar of the recapitulation.

LECTURE VIII

THERE is no accepted classification of musical forms, so we are saved the trouble of contradicting any received opinions in this matter, and we can proceed at once to build our own classification on a basis of fact.

In my last lecture I dealt with only one aspect of musical form. I may perhaps have given the impression that recapitulation was the only aspect to be considered. While it is true that musical recapitulation has a far greater scope, far more freedom, and a far profounder accuracy than is popularly supposed, it is not more than the antithesis to the equally important aspect of form which is conveniently called development. We may easily classify the forms of whole musical compositions into those which depend upon shape and those which depend upon texture. According to this classification, the shaped forms are those of the sonata, of which the main types are: the first-movement form, or sonata form *par excellence*; and the rondo, with the addition of the smaller lyric and dance forms that do not greatly transcend the scope of an alternation of a couple of lyric melodies. The texture forms are mainly represented by the fugue and by the structure of polyphonic motets and madrigals in sixteenth-century music. This classification is important and obvious in itself; but one of its chief consequences is that a fugue is, properly speaking, not a form at all, and most of the confusion and misinformation of the text-books on fugue results from setting up rules for the structure of a fugue as a whole without realizing that such rules, whoever designed them, exist for the sole convenience of teachers and pupils, and that the faint indications that the great composers comply with them are so rare as to be almost certainly accidental. I must leave it to more learned persons to discover the composers whose fugues anticipate or follow the precepts drawn up by Cherubini. The examples he provides specially for his treatise on counterpoint and fugue illustrate his rules with a bluff inaccuracy which may have some educational value as preparing students for the deceptions of real life; but the really noble fugue which he quotes from his own *Credo* is provided by him with an analysis which can be understood only as an attempt to avoid betraying trade secrets.

As for Bach, we all believe, and the belief is correct, that Bach's fugues are uniquely solid and consistent in their forms; yet we still persist in trying to analyse them according to the scheme of Cherubini, who strongly disapproved of Bach, while we completely ignore the clear classification and crystalline regularity of the examples drawn up with an avowed educational purpose by Bach himself in *Die Kunst der Fuge*.

The first step towards common sense in the matter is to recognize that as an integral art-form there is no such thing as *a* fugue. The term should be used mainly without an article, definite or indefinite. The only meaning of 'a fugue' is a composition written entirely in fugue. It is a medium like blank verse. There is no such thing as *a* blank verse, because you cannot tell that a verse is blank until you have heard a sufficient number of verses to convince you that the poet is abstaining from rhyme. *Paradise Lost* is *in* blank verse. A misguided contemporary of Milton thought that the poem would be more elegant and popular if it were made to rhyme, and Milton to save trouble derisively gave him permission to tag his verses. In one important sense this process obviously casts the whole poem into a different art-form; but the art-forms in question are textures, and the shape of the poem—that is to say, its plot and its theological, ethical, and descriptive contents— remains unaffected and undetermined by the textures.

For our present purpose it will be more convenient to consider the antithesis between texture and shape in the light of general means of expression available in various parts of all art-forms, and not as terms separating one form from another. Evidently recapitulation is a matter of shape, and development is a field in which we may expect a more prominent, or a higher, function for texture. From the point of view of a sonata movement a fugue consists entirely of development; by which I do not mean that fugue is a normal, or even safe, means of development in sonata works; but in a fugue anything like an extensive recapitulation has an effect rather subversive of fugue style. It is like the powerful device at the end of *Paradise Lost* which I cited in my last lecture, and it sadly distracts the attention of the orthodox analyst. Reams of fantastic speculation have been written on the provocation which Bach gives if he allows three bars of cadence in the dominant early in a fugue to be recognizable note for note in the tonic at the end. I must beg you not to expect me to treat such speculations with courtesy. The results of analysis will not be a nuisance if the analysis will only take each work on its own terms, and proceed from fact to fact instead of troubling to save Cherubini's face.

When the composer does purposely combine the procedures of texture with those of shape, he makes the savers of Cherubini's face dangerously angry. Bach's great E minor Organ Fugue, known as *The Wedge*, has the appalling effrontery to be in da capo form. I find myself in agreement with the comparatively naïve listener to whom the total effect of this fugue is magnificent just because of the da capo, and I can see no sense whatever in the criticisms directed against that feature. If Bach had produced a few more specimens of the kind, it might have been recognized as a classical form; and, similarly, if Beethoven had produced dozens of movements on the lines of the finale of the 'Eroica' Symphony, we should have had no nonsense about its being formless because its form happens at present to be unique. Unique such things are, and unique they must remain, for their form is their life which developed from within, and imitations of it cannot live if they are moulded from without; but this is also the case with living examples in forms that seem most conventional. As I have said elsewhere, a great composer's hundred specimens of a form may be as like as two peas without being as like as two buttons.

In the last resort, our analysis must condescend to details, and one curious consequence of this is that the only part of the old-fashioned teaching of fugue that is truly classical and well observed is that which is most tiresome for students: a tangle of finicking rules as to the difference between subject and answer, the delicate principles by which the answer is so often not an exact transposition of the subject, but a tonal, as distinct from a real, answer—a tonal reflection of the subject from the authentic into the plagal view of the octave, and vice versa.

It is impossible to draw up these rules without making allowances which force both the student and the teacher to recognize some of the finer aspects of a master's style. In the middle of the nineteenth century there appeared two volumes of canons and fugues, the posthumous work of an excellent musician, August Alexander Klengel, who arranged this *magnum opus* exactly like *Das Wohltemperirte Klavier*, from the scheme of which it differs in providing strict canons instead of free preludes. Hauptmann, his editor, said that Klengel 'expresses his own thoughts in the way in which Bach would have done had he lived at the present day'. This is a dangerous scheme, and those who deign to cast a contemptuous glance at poor Klengel's *magnum opus* are usually content to refute it by saying that Bach was a poet and that Klengel was a pedant. This is unfair to Klengel, who was no pedant and whose fugue subjects are always good and often charming. One fugue, on Mozart's *La ci darem la mano*, is no blasphemy on Mozart's theme, and makes witty use of the second movement of that duet. The real trouble with Klengel's work does not come from lack of poetry, but from lack of technique in a matter which ought not to be beyond the scrutiny of academic teaching. Klengel's phrases are permanently tagged, and not with the skill of a master of the heroic couplet, but with the flat-footed sententiousness of a schoolboy who can write grammar but cannot build a paragraph. An odd result of this is that the canons often sound actually more free than the fugues, because the exigences of canon prevent Klengel from coming to full closes with every clause.

If we are to get rid of the illusions produced by the apparent solidity and simplicity of the classical artforms, we shall find it convenient to proceed on the lines of classifying modes of form universally prevalent rather than the art-forms of pieces as wholes. A fugue is a composition which, being written in fugue, has no leisure for recapitulation, but proceeds entirely by development, its very exposition being the immediate development of the fugue subject. In the forms that have shapes as wholes the effect of symmetry is produced by recapitulation; and in such forms the three principle elements are exposition, development, and recapitulation. More particular rules of form arise as convenient procedures that secure the composer against confusion, or crosspurposes, in these elements. The business of exposition is to lay the materials clearly before us, and the general rules for this are much the same in music as in drama. In the most businesslike exposition, one idea may lead argumentatively to another; and, in fact, one of the great fallacies of an over-facile analysis, and of the habits which it stimulates in composers, is the notion that a witty concatenation of the figures of one theme with those of another constitutes a trustworthy logical connexion of ideas, and that such wit is essential to all music that claims to be important. It is much more important that the ideas put forward in an exposition should be made clear by every legitimate means of contrast than that they should be connected by argumentative wit. There are no limits to the refinement and allusiveness of style permissible in an exposition, but there are limits, inexorable in music as in drama, to the amount of argumentative procedure or development for which an exposition can find room.

In exposition and recapitulation the handling of keys, and many other technical matters, will differ from what is appropriate to development; and here we often find that modern innovators are apt to ignore the consequences implicit in their new styles, and that they are far more apt to remain hidebound by irrelevant rules which they believe to be classical than to show any real sense of the freedom which they ought to find in their new world. For instance, Reger's meticulous adherence to the external features of sonata form has much the same relation to his extremely chromatic style as a high box-seat for the driver has to the purposes of a motor-car. I frankly cannot see anything in Reger's classical forms that is more to the purpose of his highly self-conscious modern ways of moving than the shape of a converted brougham was to the purpose of the earliest motor-cars. The forms of Bruckner's symphonies are a close historic parallel to the defects of the first attempt at a great Atlantic liner, the *Great Eastern*.

The criticism that treats such defects as breaches of rule is manifestly in danger of mistaking an unprecedented quality for a mere defect; but its most serious danger is in its identity with the same confusion of thought that makes the pioneer compositions fail in their purpose. The really melancholy example of this kind of confusion is to be seen in the history of a neglected work of Schumann, which cost him a great deal of trouble and which, though disappointing as a whole, contains many beautiful ideas. He published his Second Pianoforte Sonata, in F minor, Op. 14, with the title *Concert sans Orchestre*, under the naïve delusion that its style had some of the brilliance of a pianoforte concerto. In a later edition it appears as Sonata in F minor, and has an important and typically Schumannesque scherzo. I always understood that this scherzo was the most important of the improved features of the second edition. By the way, not all the other features of the second edition are improvements: Schumann's later revisions of his works are apt to show an effort to become a more conventional person. But it is really rather shocking to find that this had always been part of the sonata, and that it was extruded from the first edition because a classical concerto, which this sonata never remotely resembled, never had, and therefore ought never to have, a scherzo. If this was the notion of classical forms prevalent in what was known as the Romantic Period, no wonder that some people behaved as though the classics ought never to have occurred.

Neither in the officially recognized history of sonata form, nor in the external appearances of the distribution and derivation of sonata themes, is it possible to discover the principles of musical form in the great composers since Bach. What passes for orthodoxy in these matters is the customs of composers for whom we no longer care; and even in these composers its real merits are not discoverable by the lines of analysis which are still regarded as orthodox. The whole terminology of the sonata form is wrong. The term 'second subject', which, by the way, is an English provincialism, has perhaps done more damage to methods of musical criticism than any other blunder in musical history. If it has not done equally serious damage to composition, that is because it is almost always effective and convenient to construct a movement with two, and not more than two, important contrasted themes stated in an exposition which assigns one to the home tonic and the other to a complementary key. The two themes will not of themselves fill the necessary space. So there is always room for supplementary passages, one group of which effects the transition between the home tonic and the complementary key, while the other completes the exposition. These passages will give effective relief most easily by being rapid, and the most convenient way to bring the rapidity to a climax which automatically stops it is to end your passage with a trill. Hence Spohr's idea of strict form.

Schumann, who shared with every sane musician of his day a great admiration for Spohr, pointed out that those critics and composers were gravely mistaken in imagining that Spohr's untroubled mastery was as easy to achieve as it seemed; but the fact remains that this regular form may be cheapened until it becomes almost fool-proof, and this is what Parry means when he says that to Beethoven brilliant passages were a byword as odious as cant to Carlyle. Nevertheless, we must not judge by appearances, and the first movements of the 'Waldstein' Sonata, which contains some of Beethoven's boldest innovations, and the third 'Rasoumovsky' Quartet are externally such perfect examples of Spohr's regular form that the chief humour of the situation is in the fact that they are exceptional in Beethoven. In any case, these are pioneer works of which the originality is not for a moment in doubt. And Spohr, as he showed in his 'Historical' Symphony, regarded himself as belonging to a later generation than Beethoven.

We shall never begin to understand the sonata style so long as we take the view that it differs from earlier styles in having two contrasted themes instead of one. It may have any number of themes. Sebastian Bach has left plenty of movements externally resembling a sonata movement with several clearly contrasted themes; and Haydn tends more and more in his later works to build his second group mainly out of the materials of his first. Philipp Emanuel Bach is supposed to be the composer who bridged the gulf between the two styles, and it seems unreasonable to doubt this when early in Haydn's career he sent a personal message to Haydn to express his delight in finding a composer who really understood him; but neither Haydn nor Philipp Emanuel Bach seems aware of Haydn's own irresistible force, unique until Mozart developed it more systematically though not more persistently, as a composer to whom every process of form was inveterately dramatic: so much so that his lyric and dance forms, as in his slow movements and scherzos, became more deeply lyric as an essentially dramatic contrast to the active forms.

The only terminology which gives safe guidance to the interpretation of classical forms consists of the three words 'exposition', 'development', and 'recapitulation'; and no formal procedure can be profitably criticized as either an example or a breach of rule except in so far as it keeps these three notions inviolate. We shall do well to distrust all plausible laws of proportion that can be applied to the length and contents of sections. One of the most plausible is that which applies the canon of the golden section, the line divided in extreme and mean ratio, to musical forms. The applications are often fascinating, but are so manifold that they can be made to prove anything. We shall have more convenient occasion to deal with them in discussing the time-dimension in music and the senses in which artistic perfection is a type of infinity. At present we may conveniently consider the criteria that unquestionably arise from the nature of exposition, development, and recapitulation. Here the analogies of drama are obvious and not misleading.

Exposition should attend to its business, and not be weakened or confused by a discursiveness that may be appropriate to development. There is nothing in this to prevent a composer from using his finest wit in an exposition, and the increase in his own practice and the accumulated weight of precedents will tend to make his style more and more allusive and witty. The later works of Haydn, Mozart, and Beethoven, and every work of Brahms from the outset, all show this tendency as clearly in their expositions as anywhere else in a movement; and this gives rise to the dangerous notion that such wit constitutes the logic of music. It is extremely dangerous to suppose that it can constitute the logic of any art. Great composers themselves can be misled by it, not in their works, but in their advice to less experienced artists. When Haydn's style had become habitual to him he reproached young composers with using an extravagant amount of material instead of seeing what they could extract from one good theme. But Haydn himself extracts an abundance of good things out of his one theme, and in this he would never have succeeded if he had not in his earlier works been one of the most extravagant composers in piling up all the good things that occurred to him.

The composer whose themes are all linked together by an outwardly logical connective tissue is neither vital nor logical except in so far as there are differences in all his identities. Nothing is more childish, or for that matter more easy, than the process of inventing, or borrowing, a single pregnant figure and relying upon twisting it into different rhythms to give logical coherence to your work. It is strange to find so great a composer as Stanford giving in his treatise on composition not only the worst possible advice to young composers, but selecting the most unfortunate example for his warning against the extravagance of using a number of different themes. The early works of all great composers, Brahms's not excepted, have relied upon a large number of different themes. Not only that, but the most experienced composer will show this and many other phenomena of an early work when late in life he handles an art-form that is new to him. It is natural to write in a large hand and to make obvious distinctions before you trust yourself with small writing and subtle lines. Stanford unfortunately cites the composers of symphonic poems as representing the bad habit of using an extravagant number of different themes. Now, if there is one doctrine more prominent than any other in the pioneer Liszt's official propaganda for his symphonic poems, it is the doctrine that the whole work should be derived from one *Urkeim*, as living texture is derived from a single nucleated cell. Liszt's derivations are ingenious, but they neither help nor hinder the continuity of his works. Great impetus was given to his doctrine by the easy and fascinating analysis of the way in which the themes of Wagner's operas are associated with his dramatic events and ideas. This association is present in such minute detail that the dreadful doctrine has arisen that Wagner's music is actually built up from leitmotive to leitmotive; as, no doubt, the Forth Bridge is constructed from rivet to rivet, and the dramas are constructed from subject to predicate, if not from syllable to syllable. In the love-scene in *Tristan* the lovers do, indeed, descend to such a pathetically profound infantility as 'Dies süsse Wörtlein "und"' ('That sweet little word "and"'). Wagner carries it off quite successfully as natural lovers' babblings, but it is only a lucky accident that has saved the passage from becoming the source of an officially recognized *und-motiv*. I have already dealt with the large-scale recapitulations which are as important a feature in Wagner's forms as in any classical symphony, and all

I need insist upon here is that it is folly to suppose that the essential structure of Wagner's music is on less particular lines than that of his drama.

When we deny that Schubert is a great master of form we ought not to mean that he breaks orthodox rules. We ought not, in fact, to suppose that his mastery of form is not potentially of the highest order. His openings are magnificent, his transition to the second group primitive and abrupt, but not necessarily wrong. His second group usually falls into a weak and ill-timed process of development; a weakness which, by the way, is not present in the 'Unfinished' Symphony, though that is one of the very cases where his cadence group is derived in Haydnesque fashion from the main theme of his second group. Altogether, the first movement of the 'Unfinished' Symphony is as perfect a masterpiece as can be found anywhere; and its abrupt transition is by no means a defect.

As Schubert's expositions are ruined by premature and discursive developments, wherein Schubert differs from Dvořák in the fact that Dvořák ruins his first group and transition in the same way, so Schubert's developments are weakened, first, by the fact that too much development has already taken place, and secondly, by two compensating tendencies: (1) to develop one of his themes into a long lyric episode with no action; and (2) to aim at a cumulative effect by simply repeating whole pages of a process in another key. I believe the inspiring cause of this to be the splendid effect which Beethoven boldly produces in the development of the 'Eroica' Symphony by the recurrence of his transition theme at two different stages in preparing for two very different kinds of development.

Schubert is usually accused of repeating himself too much. Quantitatively he does not repeat himself nearly as much as the more authoritative masters, but he is in the unfortunate position of being obliged to repeat what will not bear repetition. When he comes to his recapitulation, the inconvenience of the discursive developments in his exposition becomes painfully manifest; and only in the great C major Symphony does Schubert find himself with energy left for a big coda, and here severe critics are apt to make the easy remark that the listener's energy is less than Schubert's. Still, the defects of Schubert's form are too deeply rooted in his qualities for us to accept mere shortening with a pair of scissors as a remedy. Actually, few, if any, of Schubert's movements would be too long if he had packed his material so that exposition was exposition and development was development. If Beethoven had been given Schubert's openings he would have made the works quite as long, and would have disobeyed the advice of Haydn and Stanford by using several more entirely different themes. It is a merely superficial question whether these different themes have or have not figures in common with the main themes. The exposition of Schubert's 'Unfinished' Symphony is a masterpiece, and critics who quote its cadence subject as an example of Schubert's tendency to let development intrude into exposition only show that they do not understand what development is. This cadence phrase is aesthetically a different theme from the great tune from which it is derived.

LECTURE IX

UPON the handling of the time-dimension depends the whole sense of movement in music, from the smallest and most immediate effects of rhythm to the most extensive matters of form and contrast. In these lectures I must leave most of the immediate and detailed aspects of rhythm unexplored. The subject of rhythm as an omnipresent factor in speech and dance and everything in music that results therefrom is inexhaustible and has never been neglected. But the larger aspects of musical movement are often misunderstood in ways that give rise to methods of criticism more distinguished by strong prejudice against whole schools of classical composition than by power to stimulate and enlighten. Perhaps no general aspect of music is less understood at the present day than that of movement; and no power of classical music has been so completely lost in recent times.

According to popular prejudice, this is the age of pace. The progress of civilization, as measured in miles an hour, is alarming to some people and gratifying to business men; but the art of conveying a sense of movement in music is far more rare in our modern experiments than it is in quite conventional works on classical lines. Many of our composers and critics are quite unaware of this, and show that they simply do not appreciate a sense of movement. Others are more aware of how that sense can be stimulated, but they reject the quality of movement as representing an undignified phase through which music regrettably passed when Haydn and Mozart dramatized the art which Bach had brought to its true consummation in architectural and static majesty. Besides representing an indisputable matter of taste, this view has the advantage of being founded on fact. To a mind that has an instinctive taste for Bach and older forms of art the impact of dramatic music, if it does not come early in life, produces a disconcerting shock, and the attention is unwilling to be roused to an activity in which the sense of movement is frequently changed instead of being maintained at one steady rate. If the taste for Bach is not instinctive, but has been recently acquired, the shock may be as disagreeable as an attack upon one's religion; and if you are a composer who has discovered a knack of writing, not necessarily in Bach's art-forms, but in a style that has the same appearance of even flow, the art of Mozart, Haydn, and Beethoven, and all that is derived from those masters, may make you as furious as a tigress protecting her cubs against interference. Something like this fury inspires many intellectual fashions in music to-day. It has the weakness of all tendencies that come from being afraid of life, and such fears blind us to the deeper qualities which the things we like best share in common with all that is great and true.

Mozart is now in fashion, largely because romanticism is out of fashion. Romanticism is out of fashion because at present we are tired of the unexpected and the catastrophic, and we delight in things that are punctual, predestined, and exact. Such qualities we recognize in Bach and Mozart, and for their sake we are ready to ignore or forget Mozart's irrepressible dramatic tendencies. Before Bach attained his present popularity, the naïve listener thought him monotonous : an impression based on the indisputable fact that in Bach's forms everything reveals itself as an uninterrupted unfolding of elements already implied from the outset. It would be fair to say that in Bach much may develop, but nothing can happen. If this condition is essential to our enjoyment, the paramount symmetry and manifest system of Mozart's forms may reconcile us to the fact that in Mozart many things happen.

Before Bach became popular, the naïve lover of music had a standard of movement set by Mozart, disturbed by Haydn, raised to a higher power by Beethoven, and completely obliterated by Wagner. Bach did not reach this standard. His movement was too uniform. Current modern criticism sees that Wagner obliterated the standard, but fails to realize that he mastered a standard of his own.

Some time-elements will fill a few seconds : others will take a quarter of an hour to appear. Bach's great Organ Toccata in F ought to take eight minutes if it is not played ridiculously fast. It can be played surprisingly slowly with rather a gain than a loss to its impression of a momentum that nothing can stop; but though its whole system depends upon its having no contrasting themes, its movement constantly renews its energy by the clearest possible contrast between short phrases and long.

The sense of movement is quite independent of the sense of tempo. For artistic purposes, movement does not exist except when we have some sense of it; but our sense cannot remain enjoyable under constant irritation. It must be refreshed by being lulled to rest at times. I find it convenient to distinguish between three main types of movement. That of the highest artistic value and most immediate effect may be described as 'athletic'. Again and again, we shall find that what passes as a modern sense of pace is as unaesthetic as a millionaire snoring in his car while he leaves to the chauffeur the responsibility for evading the police. Still, we need not deny artistic value to a consciousness of movement in which we are passive rather than active. The consciousness of movement becomes impossible when the movement is on a cosmic scale. Wagner, who mastered all kinds of movement, achieved what may be called cosmic movement in his music-dramas, and such is the aspiration, conscious or unconscious, of most of the larger forms of music since Wagner. The strength of Bruckner and Sibelius lies in their attaining such movement. The weakness of Bruckner is in his uncritical and helpless retention of the externals of sonata form, for which the pace of his action is hopelessly too slow. Two things are essential to the sense of cosmic movement: firstly, it must not be reduced to lower orders of movement by the only possible kind of event that can normally give us a sense of movement at all; and secondly, it must become distinguishable from complete stagnation by the presence of the smaller forms of movement, so that we may have a standard of comparison. No catastrophe short of the Day of Judgement will make us conscious of the diurnal and orbital movements of the earth, but I for my own part owe a debt of gratitude to the excellent popular writer on astronomy, whose name I have ungratefully forgotten, who gave me an almost musical sense of cosmic movement by pointing out that, while the earth is moving in its orbit very much faster than any cannon-ball, it takes several minutes to traverse the length of its own diameter.

The movement of a masterly adagio has the same kind of momentum. Most composers fail to write slow movements, and the reason is usually because they do not realize that a phrase of given length will become four times as long if it is played four times as slowly. Slowness is bigness, immediately and constantly manifest.

The opposite mistake is still more frequent. Composers, especially nowadays, fail far more often to achieve real quickness than to flow with a dignified slowness. Mozart in the finale of his *Musikalischer Spass* already satirized his own earlier works and the common run of contemporary finales in passages which intelligently anticipate the nightmare flight of the finale of Tschaikovsky's Fifth Symphony, and of Alice with the Red Queen crying 'Faster, faster!' only to arrive at the foot of the same tree where they started. If you have not already tried this experiment, as I have suggested in my edition of Beethoven's Pianoforte Sonatas, you may be surprised to learn that in Beethoven's Sonata in D minor the single theme of the slow movement and nearly the whole exposition of the finale each fill exactly one minute. Let us proceed a little farther with the slow movement, and see how it is that Beethoven maintains in it an irresistible momentum. The opening theme closes into a transition which moves in shorter phrases. It moves to the complementary key, on the dominant of which it expands with enough dramatic suspense to delay the arrival of the second group until the right moment. The second group consists of a single self-repeating melody, moving, without change of tempo, four times as fast as the first group.[1]

Before we come to the positive elements of later styles, let us mention a few things which are impossible to Bach. We shall learn from this, amongst other things, how it was that, although Handel was by profession an opera-writer, the art of music had to wait for Gluck before opera could be reformed to genuine dramatic purpose. One of the most obvious negative features in Bach's style, and also in Handel's, is that it is impossible to end a piece of music otherwise than with a significant phrase. There is no such thing as a purely architectural feature of final chords. The nearest approach to such a feature is the Handelian interrupted cadence followed by a slow *Amen*, very rarely found in Bach. For Mozart and Haydn, when a lively piece of music ends with a theme, the effect is almost always so abrupt that it is evidently intended as a joke. Architectural final chords are so normal that a thematic feature may even be combined with them without making them the less extraneous to the real last melodic sentence. Sixteen bars of final chord are not enough

[1] Here the lecturer illustrated his point on the pianoforte by comparing the sense of movement shown in this Andante and in portions of Bruckner's Eighth Symphony.

for the Finale of Beethoven's Ninth Symphony. He needs five more—that is to say, four plus a final beat that is metrically equivalent to another four or eight—and these he accompanies with a new phrase which might quite well have been a theme in its own right. On the other hand, the first movement of the Ninth Symphony ends with extraordinary power with its most pregnant phrase; but the normal emphatic end in the Mozart-Haydn-Beethoven system is a series of themeless final chords, to which we may apply the proverb: 'it's all over but the shouting'.

Serious criticism does not begin until the critic has put away the childish habit of estimating all parts of a work of art by the prose value of their contents. It is as important for the composer as for the architect to make proper use of undecorated open spaces. One or more of our clever critics has suspected Beethoven of caricature in the final shouting of the Finale of the C minor Symphony. If I had been able to devote this whole course of lectures to discussing the time-element in music, I should have been justified in spending a whole lecture in demonstrating the perfect balance of these last chords. All that I can do to-day is to conclude with a few illustrations of the masterly handling of the time-dimension—in other words, of the sense of movement in music. I can leave Bach and earlier music out of account, because we do not suffer at the present day from any prejudices about music before 1750; but at all periods of music one of the rarest qualities has been mastery of movement, and at the present day the art of musical movement is almost entirely lost both in practice and in theory. We might as well ascribe athletic prowess to the twenty thousand spectators in a football crowd, and the energy of high speed to a passenger asleep in a motor-car, as believe that the present fashions in musical composition inculcate a sense of movement. We need no abstruse or recent science to tell us that movement and the sense of movement are relative. Whatever the actual facts of movement may be, there can be no sense of movement without change. Changes may be so frequent that the sense of interruption and obstruction may be greater than the sense of movement. You must have time to enjoy the feeling of movement at a certain pace before you are disturbed by any change, but if there is no change at all for a long time you will not have enough sense of movement to keep you awake.

The lesser masters of the sonata style were happy in the possession of an art which amounted at its lowest level to a good convention, and secured a comfortable sense of movement with enough variety to keep the listener awake. The works of Spohr and Hummel never fail to amble pleasantly, and all their paces are satisfactory. Great power they do not show; and when we descend from their dignified elevation we substitute for the genuine sense of movement the rattle-trap vivacity of Rossini's *Barbiere*, which many people consider a masterpiece of rapidity, but which represents for the most part complete stagnation. I have already cited the case of the trill at the end of a passage as a demonstration of how to stop movement by turning it into vibration, and the rattle-trap vivacity of Rossini and the Rossinians is vibration

138

and nothing else. Rossini had a great talent for composition, which not even his complete idleness could prevent from sometimes showing itself.

Imagine that you have just heard the whole introduction to Beethoven's Fourth Symphony: that it has given you time to appreciate its slow measure. With this in mind, let us listen to the impact of the quick movement that follows. The pauses, as you see, are exactly measured, the change to a quick time is measured by subdividing the main beats in halves and quarters, and the first phrases of the Allegro combine their own varieties of length with an allusion to the first impact of the new tempo. The whole first paragraph thus gives you every means of appreciating your speed of movement. You now settle down comfortably, and need no further stimulus until the drama is ready to take fresh action. Throughout the rest of the Allegro the variety of movement seems inexhaustible. For instance, a leisurely group of three two-bar phases may lead to twice four bars, and these to a sequence unexpectedly long in itself, but of steps of only a bar and a half that proceed in cross accents and thus give a sense of breathless speed in travelling straight towards a distance horizon. In contrast to the ever-varying stimulus of this exposition, the development is a delightfully comfortable non-stop run across wide open spaces, the greatest of which is the marvellous return to the home tonic.

The question of movement is not identical with the question of tempo. The slowest and most hesitating of Beethoven's slow movements, such as the great Rondo which constitutes the slow movement of the 'Harp' Quartet, op. 74, are products of the same power of movement that produces the most rapid of prestos. When we leave the great classics, the loss of power is more evident in quick movements than in slow. Many composers can, in fact, command a true sense of movement in a slow tempo though all their quicker movements are flaccid and merely vibratory. One of the most interesting cases arises when the composer superposes a slow theme over a quick tempo. Beethoven never loses movement by this. He has changed his metre in such a way that the effect of the slow theme does not slacken the sense of pace at all. We have merely settled down in comfort while we sweep over the wide open space. If Beethoven had translated Florestan's air into three-bar rhythm to correspond with the original metre, nothing would have saved the *Leonore* Overture from sagging.

Berlioz advertises with pride the *réunion des deux thèmes* in the music of Capulet's feast; but it is evident that his only real inspiration is in the magnificent melody of Romeo's love, and that the lively themes of the feast were from the outset a far from masterly jingle which is feverishly doing goose-step and has no reason for existence except as a fumbling counterpoint to the slow theme. Wagner's *Tannhäuser* Overture only dimly foreshadows his true powers, and there is a certain Salvation Army tub-thumping in the effectiveness with which the slow pilgrims' march eventually drowns the bacchanalian orgies; but already here Wagner shows more than Berlioz's grasp of the problem by introducing the pilgrims' theme in square rhythm before it obliterates the original momentum of the allegro in three-bar rhythm. You must turn to the later Wagner to see the real power with which a slow rhythm may ride sublimely over quicker rhythms that have not lost their momentum.

LECTURE X

THE relation between art and infinity is a subject for professional philosophers, and as such it ought to be well defined. I have no qualifications for dealing with it technically, but there are many aspects of it which I can understand well enough to treat as throwing light on the difference between great art and unimportant art, to say nothing of the difference between good and bad.

The first thing to note about infinity is that, like perfection, of which it is perhaps a special case, it is a quality that may be appreciated in samples. When Schweitzer tells us that Bach differs from his forerunners in attaining perfection and that perfection is more essential to music than to any other art, he does not commit himself to the view that all or any works of Bach are perfect, but he means that any representative specimen of Bach's style will show all the qualities that are necessary to a perfect work of art. I have already argued that there is nothing to prevent musical works of art from actually being perfect as wholes as well as in detail, a doctrine which I was brought up to fear as a heresy until the powerful authority of Robert Bridges removed my scruples.

The notion of infinity is at once burdensome and empty if it is taken to mean mere endlessness. This empty notion cannot be verified, either by experience or by reasoning. Of number and time we can only say that they provide in themselves no means of coming to an end; that no number can be conceived which you cannot add one to, or multiply by any other number, or raise to a higher power. The infinity of space has become less empty in the light of recent science. It is now said to be unbounded, but not infinite. I have no ambition to connect the art of music with the philosophical implications of space-time and an expanding universe. Somewhere in the course of my skimming readings of popular philosophy I have come across the *obiter dictum* that the infinities of number and time are unreal. The sense in which this is true is too deep for my purpose, but number presents in the simplest and most convenient way some of the phenomena by which you may recognize infinity from portions of convenient size, and may also see in it something more positive than mere endlessness.

Long before Mr. J. W. Dunne brought forward his serial philosophy, a type of infinity was found in the kind of trade-mark which consists of a picture of the patent article in question. If that picture is complete it will also have its trade-mark on its own small scale, and that trade-mark, if complete, will have its own flea on its back, and so *ad infinitum*. This is typical of the general truth that all the operations of arithmetic—addition, subtraction, multiplication and division, involution and evolution, &c. —can be applied to an infinity in quite a normal way except for the paradoxical result that they make no difference to it. Separate all the odd numbers from all the even numbers. Both classes remain infinite. Square numbers become more and more rare as we proceed in cataloguing them; yet there must be as many square numbers as plain, for every number can be squared. Properties of this kind can be seen to be infinite as soon as we have collected enough numbers to see them at all. Two of the right kind will be enough. The simplest logic will show that there is no means of limiting the field in which the relation is true.

Now such a property is present in one of the simplest lines that are known to be typically beautiful, the logarithmic curve. This is a curve, manifested by Nature in many a graceful tendril and constantly recurring in all forms of decoration and design, which has this property, that any given section of it will, if magnified, coincide with the next section. Your tendril starts with a little close curl; the radius of the curvature becomes greater in an increasing ratio as the spiral unfolds; the curvature never unfolds to a straight line; and, if you magnify any given section from the beginning outwards, you will find that it could be made to coincide with the next adjoining section.

Now it is one of the earliest discoveries in art that when an object is divided into two unequal portions, these proportions will give pleasure if the smaller portion is to the larger as the larger is to the whole—or, as Euclid puts it, if the line is divided in extreme and mean ratio. This proportion is so pleasing to the eye that it has always been known to artists as the 'golden section'. Many theorists have discovered it in the time-dimension of music. The search for golden sections in music can be fascinating; but, as I have said before, I am somewhat sceptical about its value when applied to the time-dimension, though I have often verified striking cases of it on paper. But there are so many ways of marking your sections in music that I doubt whether golden sections could not be found in all compositions, except those that are divided simply into aliquot parts. Moreover, one of the cardinal principles of rhythm, obeyed by all composers except perhaps Reger, is that a ritardando or an accelerando makes no difference to the proportions of phrases. If your phrase is too short a ritardando will not lengthen it. If your phrase is the right length no amount of rubato will damage it. Reger is fond of dissolving his final rhythms in a gradual ritardando which finally compels the conductor to beat sixteen to a bar instead of four. Far be it from me to deny that there is an aesthetic value in such a dissolution of rhythm, but it is entirely unreconcilable with the claim often made for Reger that he composes in golden sections and revives other Greek and classical notions of rhythm.

My interest is in the sound of music, and not in its appearance on paper. Far be it from me to inculcate a philistine scepticism about facts of musical proportion which are not at once evident to the ear, but I feel justified in disregarding rhythmic and proportional theories whose exponents betray that they do not hear some of the most important things in music that are not addressed to the eye. One of the less abstruse and more pestilent of these follies is a recent fashion of discovering that when Beethoven seems to shock us with an abrupt change of tempo he is in reality doing nothing of the kind—that, for instance, in the Adagio that so mysteriously interrupts the first movement of the Sonata op. 109 before the quick tempo has finished a single phrase, the semiquavers are exactly equal to the crotchets of the Vivace, so that there is no change of tempo at all. I have heard an otherwise fine and musicianly quartet party make sad nonsense of the Maestoso which begins and twice interrupts the first movement of Beethoven's Quartet op. 127. Their leader had discovered that one bar of the Maestoso ought to be exactly equal to four of the Allegro. It never occurred to him that the four-bar rhythm which Beethoven keeps up with such exceptional uniformity throughout his Allegro was specially designed to brace the Allegro up against the shocks of the Maestoso with its square but syncopated rhythm.

These readings of mysterious uniformities which thus flatten out the greatest dramatic features of classical music deserve no other epithet than 'silly'. They are natural to us only because modern music rarely has any sense of movement at all. Haydn, Mozart, and Beethoven knew quite well that one tempo could accelerate or slacken gradually into a different tempo. They had no conscious objection to the process, and there was nothing conventional in their preference for undisguised contrasts of tempo. The gradual change of one tempo to another has its merits and its purpose, but it does not express strength. On the contrary, its expression inevitably suggests loss of control. I have dealt already with some aspects of this matter in my last lecture, and need say no more about it here. If an artist uses a device which expresses loss of control, the strength or weakness of the device must depend on our impression of what it is that has lost control. In a powerful work an accelerando may suggest the force of a torrent rushing towards an abyss, or the force of Destiny stirring human passions beyond human control. In a weak work it will suggest no force at all, as if Destiny itself were merely a defective brake for a bicycle on a dangerous hill.

The weak handling of the time-dimension in music may suggest that spurious and empty infinity which is merely endless. The rhythms and proportions of great music carry their own evidence of infinity, though I believe that the discovery of golden sections in the time-dimension is too facile and naïve a procedure to give us a trustworthy clue in the matter. While it is my own conviction that the quality of infinity does exist in the proportions of great music, I confess myself quite unqualified to work on so difficult a philosophic plane; and I turn with relief to the lighter and more popular task of illustrating the infinity of music in matters of general style and emotional content.

Let us descend to a few crass illustrations of the difference between good and bad. The subject is relevant, because bad music, whatever else it can be, cannot be infinite; unless it is infinitely boring, and this it seldom is. If the truth must be faced, it is often amusing, sometimes intentionally and sometimes unintentionally. A matter perhaps more suitable for discussion over walnuts and port than in a serious lecture is the question whether bad good music is better than good bad music. Do not ask me to define without the aid of port, if not of walnuts, what these terms mean, but let us take it for granted that good bad music is infinitely preferable to bad good music. I refuse to yield to my natural impulse to abuse bad good music, by which I mean the vast bulk of honest well-schooled work without which the soil would never have become manured for any crop of great music; but good bad music is fair game. It is never infinite except in the most distressingly negative sense, but it is often inventive, and it can demonstrate with almost sublime simplicity and perfection what music ought not to be. Wagner, Meyerbeer's worst enemy, was quite generous in his praise of the really emotional duet at the end of the fourth act of *Les Huguenots*; and my own feeling towards Meyerbeer is sometimes a little wistful, like that of the daughter whose mother, having seen the folly of all such things as balls, would not let her see the folly of just one. For me this wistfulness might have survived through a whole Meyerbeer opera, had I as yet had the good luck to hear a first-rate performance. Nothing less will carry a sensitive musician through four hours, or one hour, of Meyerbeer's appalling style. And so I must content myself with enjoying its naughtiness in furtive glances at his scores. All art, says Aristotle, is imitation; and in all imitation there is an element of illusion which is more accurately called suggestion. The term 'suggestion' distinguishes what we may paradoxically call 'true' illusion from false. True artistic illusion does not deceive. False illusion deceives the unwary and exasperates everyone when it is found out.

Now you cannot accept a suggestion which you know to be false. Dr. Johnson, dealing with the grounds alleged for unity of place and other dramatic conventions, played skittles with volumes of pretentious nonsense by roundly asserting that the spectator of a drama is in his senses all the time, and is quite aware that he is in the theatre in London and not in Athens or on the sea-coast of Bohemia. Children resent a violation of their make-believe, not because it upsets their faith, but because they, being as much in their senses as Johnson's spectator, wish to play the game.

The artist must not suggest what is self-contradictory. If resources are manifestly present and implied by the circumstances, it is folly to behave as if their absence must be supplied by suggestion. Many would-be scholarly players make nonsense of Bach when they translate his harpsichord music on to the pianoforte. In the slow movement of the Italian Concerto, and many other harpsichord cantabiles, Bach writes for the harpsichord in a style that powerfully suggests the cantabile resources of a violin. The harpsichord can produce such a cantabile in a fascinatingly plaintive quality of tone with more actual sustaining power than you might expect. These elements, taken in connexion with the style of the music, will suggest many varieties of light and shade which the harpsichord is in reality not capable of giving. The pianoforte cannot give the harpsichord's quality of tone, but it can give the light and shade. The player who then argues that he must imitate the flat uniformity of the harpsichord is obviously misinterpreting, or failing to see, the suggestiveness of Bach's music.

One of the aspects of infinity in music is precisely this element of suggestion. There is no end to it, it is omnipresent, and any identifiable specimens will be a sample of the whole. Now let us use the inexhaustible, but crassly finite, Meyerbeer as our ideal awful example. In *Les Huguenots* we have soldiers and military bands galore in real presence. One of the famous choruses is the 'Rataplan', in which an unaccompanied chorus imitates in those inspiriting syllables the sound of side-drums and other military incitements to a breach of the peace. I ask whether it is possible to conceive a more impotent misuse of the device of suggestion, and I do not pause for a reply.

Do not expect a connected argument on the modes of infinity in music. I borrow from Andrew Bradley's lectures on Shakespeare an illustration of another category in which we may find infinity. Bradley ends his lecture upon that painful incident in Shakespeare, the rejection of Falstaff, by saying that Shakespeare has denied to Prince Hal and King Henry V the infinity which he gave to Falstaff. Manifestly, this kind of infinity is no less, if not more, clearly an aspect of perfection than any measurable arithmetical or geometrical matters of proportion. It means that the character is consistent from all points of view. We need not worry how this consistency has been attained. The shortest account of the matter is to say that the artist is inspired. This, as we have already seen, is inadequate, because there is a strong probability that inspiration is a state of mental athletic form which in itself gives no security whatever that the results may be artistically valuable. Modern Shakespearian criticism and research has removed many occasions for awestruck admiration by showing that Shakespeare was often using the most convenient means ready to hand without the slightest regard for the consistency of character which we are at such pains to vindicate by subtle analysis. This does not always affect the question, for the infinities of artistic perfection are not bounded by the artist's own calculations. A good action does not become less good because it is expedient, and only a vainglorious and self-righteous man will be unwilling to plead expediency as the ground or excuse for his noblest actions.

The character of Falstaff gives an excellent occasion for studying examples of perfection and infinity in music, because it forms the subject of two very great works and one faded semi-classic. The faded semi-classic is Nicolai's opera, *The Merry Wives of Windsor*, in which the straw-stuffed dummy of Shakespeare's perfunctory farce plays its part in an efficiently constructed and tolerably musical adaptation of that farce diluted in the cabbage-water of a German libretto. It is impossible to write an opera upon the real Falstaff, because, though the real Falstaff provides the quality of infinity to three plays in which the title-role is that of a man who must satisfy himself and us merely with the divine right of kings, it is round this royal person that the only coherent story is formed. But it is possible to do as Boito did: to put into the framework of *The Merry Wives* most of the speeches of the great Falstaff, reduce the farcical escapades by half, and let an element of lyric beauty into the intrigue of Anne Page and Fenton. The rest is Verdi's business, and the result is of a quality which I believe is still disputed in some quarters, but of which I have seen no adverse criticism that does not betray itself by inattention.

Perfect works of art have this quality of infinity,

that they cannot be compared. You cannot even say that an infinity of three dimensions is larger than one of two, though you may be allowed to say that it is of a higher order. You cannot say that the art of Beethoven is greater than that of Bach, or even than that of Mozart. You can only say that it has more dimensions; and so I dare not say that Elgar's symphonic poem—or, as he wisely calls it, symphonic study—*Falstaff* is greater than Verdi's opera: but I can confidently say that it is inexhaustible, and that both in relation to its programme and in its pure musical form it is a perfect example of music in full integrity.

The kind of criticism which I am attempting in these lectures is nothing if not practical, and I take occasion now to point out some obvious, but often neglected, conditions that are essential to the enjoyment of music. Many forms of irrelevant criticism arise from the judging of music under conditions which the critic should have avoided. Infinities and perfections are inexhaustible. This does not mean that the energy of listeners is inexhaustible. Unfortunately, one of the commonest forms of pious opinion assumes that the listener can treat his mind as no sane person would treat his digestion. I was once told by an extremely impressive connoisseur in such matters that you could, given time and money, enjoy in Paris a *dîner à trois cinqs*—that is to say, a meal which began with five courses, ranging from soup to dessert, which was followed by an interval employed I was not told how; after which there was another set of five courses, also ranging from soup to dessert and followed by another interval, concerning which my speculations were involuntary and regrettable: and the entertainment concluded by a third set of five courses. No doubt the whole enterprise was rendered possible by consummate art in the selection of the courses and the occupation of the intervals. At all events, I believe it to have been aesthetically a sounder proposition than that of Bülow, who on the excuse that opportunities for hearing Beethoven's Ninth Symphony were rare, performed it twice in succession to a single audience on a single occasion. The enterprise was quite unworthy of Bülow's intelligence. Few contrasts could be more inept than that provided by the beginning of such a work heard immediately after the end. Weingartner tells us from personal knowledge that neither the performers nor the audience were fit for the second performance.

Spohr, writing from London in 1820, said many severe things about English musicians and English audiences. His conclusion is that the English have no calling for music and no true sense of it; they pursue music, like everything else, seriously, but, as one sees with English tourists sightseeing in Italy, it is evidently more a task than an enjoyment to them, and they might as well say at the end of a concert, as they say after sightseeing in Rome, 'Thank God, we've done that!' The mere fact that they can listen attentively and seriously to a concert four hours long, and often five with a little interval, suffices to prove that the music does not penetrate into them, otherwise they would already be exhausted by the first half.

Evidently our musical taste has improved in the

last hundred years; but Spohr puts his finger upon one of the commonest errors to which the hardships of critics and the pressure of pious opinion makes us liable. It has sometimes been said that such-and-such a piece can remain enjoyable after the appalling test of hundreds of hearings of it in a competition festival. This is a very dangerous claim to make; and, while I am quite certain that many of the greatest things in art will fail to stand such a hideous test, I am by no means sure that bad things under such a strain will not pass quickly through a disgusting phase and become inoffensive and eventually quite amusing. Perhaps four-fifths of the bad and inattentive criticism in this world comes from the critic's neglect of the most elementary precautions in the treatment of his musical digestion. In an art that moves in the time-direction these precautions are especially necessary, and when the real existence of the art is in performance the chances of criticizing a work from a wrong point of view are multiplied indefinitely.

Many technical problems arise which have only an indirect connexion with the merits of the work. Take, for example, Glazounov's famous three types of orchestration: the first-class work which sounds well when read at sight and magnificent when properly rehearsed; the second-class work that does not sound well on a first reading, but can be made to sound well with practice; and the third-class work that cannot be made to sound well with any amount of rehearsal. Whatever perfection may be consistent with this view of orchestration, it has no touch of infinity. Every composer, from Beethoven, Wagner, and Strauss to the possessors of the merest rudiments of common sense, will agree with Glazounov and Rimsky-Korsakov that the first type of orchestration is the thing at which he should consciously and conscientiously aim; but Rimsky-Korsakov, to whom Beethoven is as contemptible as an obsolete motor-car, has not the faintest glimmering of a kind of orchestration which sounds infamous at a first rehearsal, but which, like Beethoven's, becomes magnificent when properly practised. The art by which its magnificence can be revealed is by no means capable of making good orchestration out of bad. I have more than once been rebuked for defending many errors of Beethoven's scoring by pointing out that with double wind, such as was by no means unknown to Beethoven and even to Mozart, it becomes a merely financial matter to realize Beethoven's intentions. I have been told that on these lines all bad scoring could be corrected. But this is simply not true. Bad scoring is unimaginative, and no amount of correction will make it imaginative. Moreover, there is plenty of bad scoring which is ostensibly correct. To that end the rules of part-writing have been made. If you obey the rules, you can save yourself the trouble of using your imagination at all; or, if you do not wish to indulge in so sublime a self-renunciation, you may let your imagination wallow in the self-satisfaction of a prosperous person I once heard of who, when a young artist who eventually became President of the Royal Academy was holding forth on the importance of imagination in art, broke in with the illuminating comment: 'You are quite right there, sir. It's a wonderful thing, imagination. Sometimes of a quiet evening when I've nothing better to do I sit in front of the fire imagining, and imagining, and imagining, until I feel quite stoopid.'

I am not sure that this gentleman never had a glimpse of the infinite. His frame of mind evidently included a wholesome capacity for the bewilderment which perfection and infinity must inspire. Certainly there is an incalculable element in all great art. The only danger in identifying perfection and infinity with the incalculable is that we may deny all three titles to art in which we find ourselves able to calculate at all. Herein I am compelled to join issue with one of Sir Henry Hadow's illustrations in the *Oxford History of Music*. He compares the opening of Mozart's great C major Quintet with that of Beethoven's first 'Rasoumovsky' Quartet, and says that Beethoven has added the element of the incalculable; thus denying it by implication to Mozart's opening. Now the only real resemblance between Mozart's opening and Beethoven's is that both openings agree in giving a theme to the violoncello below a long expanse of chords repeated in quaver movement. Obvious points of difference are that Beethoven is writing a tune, while Mozart is explicitly stating a formula. In its original statement, Mozart's formula must remain calculable long enough to express its meaning at all. Beethoven's opening is not a formula, but a tune. As such it is in four-bar rhythm instead of Mozart's already irregular five bars, and Beethoven's art would become painfully calculable if he allowed this tune to finish itself symmetrically. His procedure is incalculable, simple, and bold. But

I cannot see that in the long run Mozart's procedure is less incalculable. I see nothing calculable in the way in which his formula drifts into a melodic phrase which rounds off the first paragraph with a half-close; and when after an impressive pause he begins a counterstatement in the minor with the parts of violin and violoncello interchanged, no doubt I find myself saying that this is just what I expected, but I am certainly being wise after the event: and so with every later step in the music. One infinity is as great as any other, and if this example of Mozart at his highest power seems to us more calculable than Beethoven's, that is merely the illusion that comes from our being more familiar with Mozart's formulas. Note that we must not say that the difference lies in Mozart's using formulas and Beethoven's using none. The work that uses formulas is quite as incalculable as the work which places all its distinction in its themes. Mozart's three greatest symphonies illustrate this clearly. The E flat Symphony presents us with euphony in its clearest form, the G minor Symphony presents us with highly individual themes, and the last Symphony, miscalled 'Jupiter', makes a special point of presenting us with architectural formulas and decorative tags. There are plenty of works of Beethoven later than the first 'Rasoumovsky' which are as ostentatious as the 'Jupiter' Symphony in their avoidance of any but the commonest formulas in their themes.

No composer who believed, like Spohr and like our most facile critics, in the necessity for distinction as a quality in their themes would have started work at all upon what turns out to be one of the most

imaginative and mysterious of all Beethoven's movements, the first movement of the so-called 'Harp'
Quartet, op. 74. The one theme that shows any
character in that movement is not developed at all,
except for a few bars at the end of the recapitulation.
If you ask in what sense the movement has any
ideas, the only possible answer is that the ideas
cover the whole movement. It may be possible to
discover a relation between the composer's preference
for such formulas and some special condition of
tone-colour or romantic mystery. Certainly Mozart
handles wind instruments with special affection, and
writes a considerable number of important works
for them. All these important works show a decided
preference for formulas as distinguished from more
individual themes, and we can easily infer from this
that the formulas are preferred because they do not
distract attention from the peculiar qualities and
resources of wind tone. In this connexion it is
significant that Beethoven's 'Harp' Quartet is pre-
eminently a marvel of tone-colour. Of course, there
is no reason why marvels of tone-colour should
not also coincide with marvels of thematic invention,
but I am by no means sure that a composer's thematic
invention is not as much at its height when he produces formulas as when he is producing attractive
melodies or pregnant figures.

One of Beethoven's most allusive works is the
Overture *Zur Weihe des Hauses*. I have often produced it at Reid concerts, and have provided a single
short paragraph for it in my analytical programme.
When I recently collected my programme notes for
the Oxford University Press I decided to make a

full analysis of this overture, and was amazed at the difficulty of the task. The first four bars consist of introductory chords. And I found that quite a long argument was needed to demonstrate the exact rightness of these. I had eventually to fall back upon an awful example from the much maligned Spohr, who in the Adagio of his Ninth Concerto threw off with fatal facility some introductory chords outwardly resembling these that had probably caused Beethoven even more trouble to create than they caused me to describe.

I cannot hope to give you an impression of a coherent and well-rounded treatment of perfection and infinity but I can end these lectures with a few illustrations of a game which you may find profitable to play, either in solitude or in company. It suggested itself to me as a development of a game often played by the late Julius Röntgen, who would strike a single chord, or two chords, and ask you to guess the work of which it was the beginning. This is often easier than you might expect. There is a pathetic story of a man who had composed a great opera, and who after much wire-pulling had secured an audition limited to four hours with the intendant and the conductor of a certain theatre. He came to the audition with his skyscraper score and struck the first chord, whereupon the conductor and the intendant and the leading critics with one impulse cried '*Meistersinger!*' and therewith concluded the audition.

You may be in some doubt whether the E flat chord, struck without much percussion, is or is not the opening of Beethoven's Quartet, op. 127; but you can have no doubt that this pair of chords is the opening of Schumann's Quintet; or that the E flat triad in this position, without a fifth, is the opening of Beethoven's E flat Concerto. But a more interesting variety of the game is to proceed farther, and, instead of inquiring the title of the piece, to put yourself in the position of a naïve listener and to ask at what point you can recognize that you are dealing with an extraordinary work. With great music this will reveal itself at exactly the right time. You cannot reasonably expect a formal opening to reveal at once whether the composer is more than a master of the formula. As you listen to the opening of the 'Jupiter' Symphony, you at once recognize the formula, the typical stage gesture of the tyrant on his throne and the suppliant pleading at his feet. As the music proceeds, you recognize the excellent proportions, as of a street designed by the brothers Adam; and you also recognize in the instrumentation that the building materials are of excellent quality: but when the counterstatement begins you draw a long breath of satisfaction and evident expectation that this artist is equal to anything.

Take the opposite case of a work which begins with an obviously pregnant statement. Here what is in question will be the composer's capacity to construct anything more important than a collection of epigrams. In his early works Beethoven sometimes leaves us in doubt. The G major Quartet begins beautifully and wittily, but remains for an unusually long time without signs that it is capable of sustained effort; but even in his earliest work Beethoven never failed to overcome his nervous abruptness, and to pass from a sententious manner to a power of sustained phrasing that is evidently capable of anything.

Composers since Wagner have often emulated, with not very frequent success, his power of cosmic movement in a vast musical time-space. As the monodists already discovered at the beginning of the seventeenth century, nothing is easier than to produce a cumulative effect by dwelling on one chord and repeating a single figure *ad infinitum*. How are we to know that the creator of the opening of *Rheingold* is a wiser artist than a dear old gentleman whom my contemporary Oxonians remember as a butt of musical undergraduate wit, who came back from Bayreuth saying in his broad dialect that he did not see why they made such a fuss about the prelude to *Rheingold* being all on a chord of E flat, inasmuch as he had quite independently prefaced his own oratorio of *Jonah* with a prelude entirely on the chord of D, representing, I suppose, the interior of Jonah's whale?

Let us conclude our view of musical infinity by taking the opening of *Rheingold* and ascertaining the point at which we can see that Wagner was no fool.

PRINTED BY
JARROLD AND SONS, LTD.
NORWICH